BEETHOVEN

A Character Study together with
Wagner's Indebtedness to Beethoven

GEORGE ALEXANDER FISCHER

1st WORLD
LIBRARY
Literary Society

Beethoven

George Alexander Fischer

© 1st World Library, 2009
PO Box 2211
Fairfield, IA 52556
www.1stworldlibrary.com
First Edition

LCCN: 2009923385

Softcover ISBN: 978-1-4218-8835-4
Hardcover ISBN: 978-1-4218-8934-4
eBook ISBN: 978-1-4218-8736-4

Purchase *"Beethoven"*
as a traditional bound book at:
www.1stWorldLibrary.com/purchase.asp?ISBN=978-1-4218-8835-4

1st World Library is a literary, educational organization
dedicated to:

- Creating a free internet library of downloadable ebooks

- Hosting writing competitions and offering book publishing
scholarships.

Interested in more 1st World Library books? contact:
literacy@1stworldlibrary.com
Check us out at: www.1stworldlibrary.com

1st World Library Literary Society

Giving Back to the World

"If you want to work on the core problem, it's early school literacy."

- James Barksdale, former CEO of Netscape

"No skill is more crucial to the future of a child, or to a democratic and prosperous society, than literacy."

- Los Angeles Times

"Literacy... means far more than learning how to read and write... The aim is to transmit... knowledge and promote social participation."

- UNESCO

"Literacy is not a luxury, it is a right and a responsibility. If our world is to meet the challenges of the twenty-first century we must harness the energy and creativity of all our citizens."

- President Bill Clinton

"Parents should be encouraged to read to their children, and teachers should be equipped with all available techniques for teaching literacy, so the varying needs and capacities of individual kids can be taken into account."

- Hugh Mackay

Es kann die Spur von meinen Erdentagen Nicht in Aeonen untergehn.

—GOETHE.

TO THE MEMORY OF

MY FATHER

CONTENTS

CHAPTER I

EARLY PROMISE

God acts upon earth only by means of superior chosen men.

—HERDER: *Ideas Toward a History of Mankind.*

As life broadens with advancing culture, and people are able to appropriate to themselves more of the various forms of art, the artist himself attains to greater power, his abilities increase in direct ratio with the progress in culture made by the people and their ability to comprehend him. When one side or phase of an art comes to be received, new and more difficult problems are invariably presented, the elucidation of which can only be effected by a higher development of the faculties. There is never an approach to equilibrium between the artist and his public. As it advances in knowledge of his art, he maintains the want of balance, the disproportion that always exists between the genius and the ordinary man, by rising ever to greater heights.

If Bach is the mathematician of music, as has been asserted, Beethoven is its philosopher. In his work the philosophic spirit comes to the fore. To the genius of the musician is added in Beethoven a wide mental grasp, an altruistic spirit, that seeks to help humanity on the upward path. He addresses the intellect of mankind.

Up to Beethoven's time musicians in general (Bach is always an exception) performed their work without the aid of an intellect for the most part; they worked by intuition. In everything outside their art they were like children. Beethoven was the first one having the independence to think for himself—the first to have ideas on subjects unconnected with his art. He it was who established the dignity of the artist over that of the simply well-born. His entire life was a protest against the pretensions of birth over mind. His predecessors, to a great extent subjugated by their social superiors, sought only to please. Nothing further was expected of them. This mental attitude is apparent in their work. The language of the courtier is usually polished, but will never have the virility that characterizes the speech of the free man.

As with all valuable things, however, Beethoven's music is not to be enjoyed for nothing. We must on our side contribute something to the enterprise, something more than simply buying a ticket to the performance. We must study his work in the right spirit, and place ourselves in a receptive attitude when listening to it to understand his message. Often metaphysical, particularly in the work of his later years, his meaning will be revealed only when we devote to it earnest and sympathetic study. No other composer demands so much of one; no other rewards the student so richly for the effort required. The making a fact the subject of thought vitalizes it. It is as if the master had said to the aspirant: "I will admit you into the ranks of my disciples, but you must first prove yourself worthy." An initiation is necessary; somewhat of the intense mental activity which characterized Beethoven in the composition of his works is required of the student also.

There is a tax imposed for the enjoyment of them.

Like Thoreau, Beethoven came on the world's stage "just in the nick of time," and almost immediately had to begin hewing out a path for himself. He was born in the workshop, as was Mozart, and learned music simultaneously with speaking. Stirring times they were in which he first saw the light, and so indeed continued with ever-increasing intensity, like a good drama, until nearly his end. The American Revolution became an accomplished fact during his boyhood. Nearer home, events were fast coming to a focus, which culminated in the French Revolution. The magic words, Liberty, Equality, Fraternity, and the ideas for which they stood, were everywhere in the minds of the people. The age called for enlightenment, spiritual growth.

On reaching manhood, he found a world in transition; he realized that he was on the threshold of a new order of things, and with ready prescience took advantage of such as could be utilized in his art. Through Beethoven the resources of the orchestra were increased, an added range was given the keyboard of the piano, the human voice was given tasks that at the time seemed impossible of achievement. He established the precedent, which Wagner acted on later, of employing the human voice as a tool, an instrument, to be used in the exigencies of his art, as if it were a part of the orchestra.

Beethoven's birthplace, Bonn, no doubt proved a favorable soil for the propagation of the new ideas. The unrest pervading all classes, an outcome of the Revolution, showed itself among the more serious-minded in increased intellectuality, and a reaching after higher things. This *Zeitgeist* is clearly reflected in his compositions, in particular the symphonies and sonatas. "Under the lead of Italian vocalism," said Wagner, speaking of the period just preceding the time of which we write, "music had become an art of sheer agreeableness." The beautiful in music had been sufficiently exploited by Mozart and Haydn. Beethoven demonstrated that music has a higher function than that of mere beauty, or the simple act of giving pleasure. The beautiful in literature is not its best part. To the earnest thinker, the seeker after truth, the student who looks for illumination on life's problem, beauty in itself is insufficient. It is the best office of art, of Beethoven's art in particular, that it leads ever onward and upward; that it acts not only on the esthetic and moral sense, but develops the mental faculties as well, enabling the individual to find a purpose and meaning in life.

* * * * *

Ludwig van Beethoven was born at Bonn, December 16, 1770. He came of a musical family. His father and grandfather were both musicians at Bonn, at the Court of the Elector of Cologne. The family originally came from Louvain, and settled in Antwerp in 1650, from which place they moved to Bonn.

This old city on the Rhine, frequently mentioned by Tacitus, older than Christianity, the scene of innumerable battles from Roman times up to the beginning of the nineteenth century, has much that is interesting about it, but is distinguished chiefly on account of having been Beethoven's birthplace. It was for five centuries (from 1268 to 1794) in the possession of the Electors of Cologne. The last one of all, Max Franz, who succeeded to the Electorate when Beethoven was fourteen years of age, and who befriended him in various ways was, in common with the entire Imperial family, a highly cultivated person, especially in music. He was the youngest son of Maria Therese, Empress of Austria, herself a fine singer and well versed in the music of the time. The Elector played the viola and his chief interest in life seems to

George Alexander Fischer

have been music. In Beethoven's time and long before, the aristocracy led lives of easy, complacent enjoyment, dabbling in art, patronizing music and the composers, seemingly with no prevision that the musicians whom they attached to their train, and who in the cases of Mozart and Haydn were at times treated but little better than lackeys, were destined by the irony of fate to occupy places in the temple of fame, which would be denied themselves.

Ludwig van Beethoven, the grandfather of the composer, received his appointment as Kapellmeister at Bonn in March of 1733, then twenty-one years of age. A little more than a century afterward a statue was erected there in the Muenster Platz to his illustrious grandson, Liszt being the moving spirit in the matter. The grandfather was in every way a worthy man, but he died when our composer was three years of age, and from that time poverty and hardship of all kinds was the portion of the family. Beethoven's father was careless and improvident. His salary of 300 florins, about $145, was all they had upon which to live. The mother was the daughter of a cook and the widow of a *valet de chambre* to one of the Electors. She was kind-hearted, of pleasant temper and lovable disposition, and the affection between mother and son was deep and lasting. The father was stern, and a strict disciplinarian, as so often happens in such cases. He was determined that the son should do better than himself, being willing to furnish the precept, if not the example.

Reared in this school of adversity the boy had a hard life. His father was his first teacher, teaching him both violin and clavier. He began with him as early as his fourth year; he seems to have been aware of the boy's ability, but had no consideration, and was a hard taskmaster. Before he was nine years of age, however, the boy's progress was so great that the father had no more to teach him.

In those times the musical life centered about the Court. Beethoven studied the organ under the court organist, Van den Eeden, an old friend of his grandfather's. Van den Eeden was succeeded shortly after by Christian Neefe, and Beethoven, then eleven years of age, was transferred to him. Neefe had an important bearing on Beethoven's life. He was in his best years, thirty-three, when he began teaching him, and was a thorough musician, who had had a varied experience before assuming this post. He was a university man as well, and it was fortunate for Beethoven in every way that he was brought in childhood under the influence of so cultivated and enthusiastic a musician. Neefe saw the boy's talent and became his friend. On one occasion the Elector took his musicians to Muenster where he had a palace, Neefe's duties requiring that he go with them. Beethoven, then under twelve years of age, was left behind as organist. Frimmel states that Neefe, on assuming the position, reserved the privilege of absenting himself frequently from his post, on condition that he provide a substitute. After the Muenster episode, the twelve-year-old Beethoven became the regular substitute. When we consider the important role that church music played in those times, such precocity is remarkable. This connection with church music bore good fruit in later years.

Neefe was soon after promoted, the Elector giving him charge of the secular as well as the sacred music of the Court, upon which Beethoven received his first appointment, that of cembalist of the orchestra. The duty of the cembalist is to preside at the piano. Only a good musician would be capable of filling such a position, as all the accompaniments were played from the score. He held this for two years, afterward playing viol in the orchestra for several years more. This work in the orchestra was later of the greatest possible benefit to him in composing. There was no salary at first, but the post had an important bearing on his life, as he was obliged to attend all the rehearsals as well as the performances of the opera, always taking an active part. Before he reached the age of fifteen he was appointed second court organist. During this year he studied the violin with Franz Ries, which enabled him a few years later to play in the band.

It was in Beethoven's fifteenth year that he played the organ every morning at the six o'clock mass in the Minorite church. For some years before and during this period he was busy trying his hand at musical composition, but nothing which he composed during his youth amounts to much. He could improvise in a marvelous manner and he attracted much attention by the exercise of this talent, becoming famous in this connection long before he was known as a composer.

His creative talent unfolded itself slowly. He had high ideals and worked faithfully toward their attainment. Failure to reach the level of his aspirations did not dishearten him; rather it spurred him on to greater effort.

The discerning intellect is always in advance of the creative. His delight in Bach was great; he studied him to such purpose that, at twelve years, he was able to play the greater part of the Well-tempered Clavichord. His wonderful interpretation of Bach, later, on his arrival in Vienna, immediately placed him in the front rank of *virtuosi*, according to Huettenbrenner, Schubert's friend.

As a boy he was docile, shy and reserved, caring nothing for the ordinary games of boys, or at least not participating in them to any extent. At an age when other boys begin learning their games, he began in composition, being forced to it, no doubt, by his father. He is said to have written a cantata at the age of ten to the memory of an English friend of the family, who died early in the year 1781. Some variations on a march in C minor bear the following statement: *Composees par un jeune amateur L v B age de dix ans.*

From year to year he kept on in musical composition, feeling his way, not discouraged by his inability to produce anything great, although Mozart's precocity and genius were no doubt frequently held up to him by others as an example to profit by. When he was seventeen he went to Vienna, the funds for the trip probably being furnished by the Elector. Here he met Mozart, then at the height of his fame, whose operas were frequently produced in Bonn and throughout Germany. He probably had some lessons from him. Mozart was very much occupied with the approaching production of Don Giovanni, which took place in Prague shortly after the young man's arrival. As Beethoven's visit terminated in three months, it is not likely that he derived much benefit from these lessons. On his first meeting with the master he extemporized for him on a subject given him by Mozart. That this was a momentous occasion to the impressionable Beethoven is certain. The emotions called up by the meeting enabled him to play with such effect that when he had finished, the well-known remark was elicited from Mozart: "Pay attention to him. He will make a noise in the world some day."

Beethoven, however, was compelled to return to Bonn, owing to the serious illness of his mother, who died of consumption July 17, 1787. He now took charge of the family and had a hard life from almost every point of view, his one enjoyment probably being in the exercise of his art. The affection between mother and son was one of the few bright spots in a boyhood of toil and privation. The father's harshness served to accentuate the kindness of the mother, and he felt her death keenly. He gave a few lessons, most unwillingly, the money from which, together with his salary as assistant organist and a portion of the father's salary, kept the family together, affording them some degree of comfort.

His return, no doubt, retarded his artistic development. The musical atmosphere of Vienna would have been much better for him, especially at this period, when he was entering manhood and eager to get at the works of contemporary composers. In those times only a small amount of the music that was written, was published. Many of the lesser works were composed merely to grace some social function, with but little thought given them as to their ultimate fate. It was customary to play from manuscript, copies of which were not readily attainable. In a city like Vienna new music was constantly being produced, occasionally at public concerts, but most often at social gatherings. The freemasonry existing among musicians and the wealthy amateurs was such that a musician of any talent was sure to be received, and put on a friendly footing. No other city in Europe afforded such opportunities for musical culture as did Vienna. It was the home of Mozart and Haydn and a host of lesser composers, as well as instrumentalists and singers. Music in one form or another was the chief diversion of the better classes, the wealthier of whom maintained their private orchestra. Many of these latter were fine performers, taking part regularly in the concerts given by their orchestras.

The next year we find Beethoven taking his meals at the Zehrgarten, where artists, professors from the university, and other notable people congregated. It was at this period that he made the acquaintance of Count Ferdinand Waldstein, the first of the aristocratic circle of friends which surrounded him all his life. Count Waldstein at twenty-four, on coming of age, entered the Germanic order, passing the year of his novitiate at the Court of the Elector at Bonn. The senior by eight years, his influence over Beethoven was considerable, as is evidenced in many ways. The Count was an enthusiastic amateur, visiting him frequently. He gave him a piano, and was useful to him in many ways. The social position of Count Waldstein was such that his friendly attitude toward Beethoven at once attracted the attention of others to the young musician. From this time on he was able to choose his friends from among the best people of his native city. The young man commemorated the friendship by taking an air of the Count's, who was somewhat of a composer, and composing twelve variations for four hands for the piano from it. Later, in 1805, after the Eroica Symphony and Fidelio, when the master had become famous, he composed the great Waldstein Sonata, opus 58, and dedicated it to him. The Waldstein family became extinct with Ferdinand, but the name will live for centuries through these compositions.

About the time of his first meeting with Count Waldstein, Beethoven made another acquaintance, which had an important bearing on his subsequent life. This was Von Breuning. He and Beethoven took violin lessons of Franz Ries. Stephen von Breuning liked Beethoven from the start and introduced him at his mother's house. The Breunings were in good circumstances, cultivated, good-natured and hospitable. They delighted in having him about, and treated him with the utmost consideration. Madame von Breuning formed a sincere, motherly affection for him; he was soon on a footing in their house almost equal to that of a member of the family. He went with them about this time on a visit to some of their relations in another city. They were instrumental in shaping his destiny in various ways, and their friendship was of great moment to him throughout life. Beethoven, then in his eighteenth year, gave lessons to the daughter Eleonore, as well as to the youngest son, Lenz. Eleonore afterward married Dr. Wegeler, who was in the same circle. Many years later he collaborated with Ries's son Ferdinand in writing reminiscences of the master.

The names of Count Waldstein and the Von Breunings are

indelibly associated with Beethoven's name as friends from the beginning. When we consider how every circumstance of Beethoven's family and mode of life tended against his forming desirable friendships, how rough in exterior and careless of his appearance he was, we can ascribe it only to the force of his character that he should have the friendship of such people. He had done nothing as yet to lead people to believe that he would ever become a great composer. As has been stated, however, he was a pianist of great originality, with a remarkable talent for improvising, which, no doubt, had much to do in making him a welcome guest wherever he went.

Madame von Breuning, with her woman's tact, and the fine intuitive perceptions that were characteristic of her, looked after his intellectual development, and was helpful to him in various ways, encouraging him as well in his musical studies. But Beethoven was by no means an easy person to get along with, as she soon found out. He was fiery and headstrong, disliking all restraint, being especially impatient of anything that savored of patronage. She seems to have known that in Beethoven she had before her that rarest product of humanity, a man of genius, and had infinite patience with him. His dislike for teaching was pronounced, then, as in after years, and she was often at her wits' end to get him to keep his engagements in this respect. She, in short, did for Beethoven what Madame Boehme did for Goethe many years before, when the poet left his native Frankfort and came to Leipsic. He was but sixteen, and found in her a friend, counsellor, almost a mother, who not only instructed him about dress and deportment, which soon enabled him to obliterate his provincialism, but showed a motherly solicitude for him, which must have been of great help to him in many ways.

Madame von Breuning interested Beethoven in the classics,

as well as in contemporary philosophical literature. Lessing, Goethe and Schiller became favorite authors with him. A much-thumbed translation of Shakespeare was a valued part of his small library in after years. He devoted much study to Homer and to Plato. Beethoven left school at the age of thirteen, and could not have given much time to his studies even when at school, as so much was required of him in his music. He learned a little—a very little, of French, also some Latin and Italian, and made up for his deficiencies by studying at home. Intellectual gifts were valued by the Von Breunings; to the youth, in his formative period, association with people like these was an education in itself.

About this time the Elector enlarged the sphere of his musical operations by establishing a national opera at Bonn, modeled after the one maintained by his imperial brother at Vienna. The works were produced on a good scale, and some excellent singers were engaged. Beethoven was appointed to play the viola, and this connection with the orchestra was of inestimable value to him in many ways. It not only gave him a knowledge of orchestration; it also made him familiar with the noted operas, which must have been greatly enjoyed by him. Mozart's operas were given a prominent place in the *repertoire*, and many others that were noteworthy were introduced. But it was not opera alone which was being performed; the drama was also represented, and his connection with the orchestra gave him an intimate acquaintance with the masterpieces of literature, which greatly influenced his subsequent career. The tragedies of Shakespeare were occasionally produced, special prominence, however, being given to the works of the great Germans, Lessing, Schiller and other philosophers and poets of the Fatherland, the exalted sentiments and pure intellectuality of which are unmatched by any people. This early acquaintance with the best literature of his time gave him an intellectual bias which served him well all his life. It is fortunate that his opportunity came so early in life, when the activity of the brain is at its highest and when lasting impressions are produced. The mental pictures called up by the portrayal of these tragedies came to the surface again in after years sublimated, refined, in symphony and sonata, in mass and opera. Every one of his works has its own story to tell; sometimes it is just the record of the events of a day as in the Pastoral Symphony, but told with a glamour of poetry and romance, that for the time gives us back our own youth in listening to it; sometimes it is a tragedy which is unfolded, as in the Appassionata Sonata or the Fifth Symphony; or it will be a Coriolanus Overture, that seething, boiling ferment of emotion and passion, the most diverse, contradictory, unlike, that can be imagined. From these impressions, acquired in the ardor of youth, when the intellect grasps at knowledge and experience with avidity, when its capacity is at its greatest, and the whole world is laid under contribution, came a rich harvest which untold generations may enjoy. No one of the many that made up the audiences night after night, probably ever formed a guess at what was going on in the brain of this quiet reserved youth during the progress of these plays. The keen discriminating intelligence which was always sifting and sorting these pictures and stowing them away for use in after years,—the flashes of enthusiasm,—the intuitive discernment of intellectual subtleties that brought him into *rapport* with the author and gave him the perception of being on an equality with the great ones of the earth, here were forces already in operation which were destined to influence the world for generations to come. To fall from this ideal world of the intellect and the emotions, at the cue of the conductor, back to the cognitions of ordinary life, and a realization of its limitations, must have been as tragic an experience to this youth, who said of himself: "I live only in my art," as any he had seen depicted on the stage. Mental processes like these write their lines deeply on the faces of gifted people.

Of the thirty-one members of the orchestra some had already attained fame, and others achieved it in after years. In this collection of geniuses the attrition of mind on mind must have been of benefit to each. The conductor, Joseph Reicha, had a nephew, Anton Reicha, whom he adopted, who played the flute in the orchestra. He and Beethoven were intimate, and the prominence which Beethoven gives to the flute in his orchestral works may in part be explained by this intimacy. Reicha afterward joined Beethoven at Vienna, remaining there until 1808, when he took up his residence in Paris. He was a prolific composer and the author of numerous theoretical works. Many of his operas were produced in Paris during his lifetime. He taught at the Paris Conservatoire, and was a member of the Institute. Then there was Bernhard Romberg, and his cousin Andreas Romberg. The latter was a musical prodigy, having played the violin in concerts as early as his seventh year. At seventeen, his virtuosity was such that he was engaged for the Concerts Spirituels at Paris. Some years later he journeyed to Bonn to be near his cousin Bernhard, with whom he was intimate, and accepted a position in the Elector's orchestra as violinist. He later went to Vienna, then Hamburg, and afterward became Kapell-meister at Gotha. He composed all kinds of music, instrumental and vocal, symphonies, operas, etc. His setting of Schiller's "Song of the Bell" is well known at the present day, as well as the oratorio, "The Transient and the Eternal." He was made Doctor of Music by Kiel University. Bernhard Romberg was a distinguished violoncellist. When his connection with the Elector's orchestra ceased, he made a professional tour to Italy and Spain with his more famous cousin Andreas and was very successful. In 1796 they came to Vienna and gave a concert at which Beethoven assisted. Bernhard afterward was a professor in the Paris Conser-vatoire and later became Kapellmeister at Berlin. He was a composer of operas, concertos, etc. While he and Beethoven were not in accord on the subject of musical composition, each disliking the other's works, there is no question but that his proximity to him at Bonn, was one of the forces that had much to do with Beethoven's artistic development.

Then there was Franz Ries, pupil of Salomon, the distinguished violinist. Ries had already achieved fame in Vienna as soloist, and had been before the public since childhood. He was Beethoven's teacher, as stated. We must not forget Neefe, Beethoven's former teacher, who was pianist, or Simrock, all of whom formed a galaxy of *virtuosi* and composers unequalled by any similar organization. Beethoven greatly profited by his association with these chosen spirits, assimilating their experiences and endeavoring to emulate them.

Thus passed a few years pleasantly enough during this formative period at Bonn, music in one form or another taking up most of his waking moments. He fell in love a few times, first with a Mlle. de Honrath of Cologne, who visited the Von Breunings frequently and was their intimate friend. She had a bright, lively disposition, and like a true daughter of Eve, took great pleasure in bantering him. There was also a Miss Westerhold who made a deep impression on him. Both were the subject of conversation by him in after years.

The visit of Haydn, who with Salomon made a short sojourn at Bonn, on their return from London to Vienna in July of 1792, gave Beethoven an opportunity for an interview with the great master, which had an important bearing on the young man's career. Salomon was acquainted with the Beethovens as he was a native of Bonn. The fame of the young musician had reached his ears, and he brought about the meeting with Haydn. Beethoven at twenty-two, had, unlike so many promising children, fulfilled the promise of his youth. He was not only a distinguished performer: his compositions were also attracting attention in his circle. In honor of the distinguished guests, a breakfast was arranged at Godesburg, a resort near Bonn, at which some compositions of Beethoven's were performed by the Elector's orchestra. Some of this music had been submitted to the master previously. Haydn, who was in holiday humor, seems to have been specially attracted to it, and encouraged Beethoven to continue.

Some of the sketch-books of the Bonn period are in the British Museum, and an examination of them is of interest as it shows his method of composing. Beethoven all through life was a hard worker and a hard taskmaster to himself. He elaborated and worked over his first inspiration, polishing, cutting down, altering, making additions, never satisfied, always aiming after the attainment of his highest ideals, never considering himself, always placing his art first and personal comfort and convenience afterward. This is apparent in the sketch-books of this early date. His industry was extraordinary, although his work grew but slowly. It was elaborated bit by bit in much the same way in which Nathaniel Hawthorne built up his romances.

Haydn's approbation was an important link in the chain of circumstances that was soon to enable Beethoven to leave for Vienna. Count Waldstein was the moving spirit in this matter, the Elector furnishing the funds. He knew that the artistic atmosphere of Vienna would be of incalculable benefit to Beethoven and encouraged him in the project. Accordingly we find him setting out for Vienna in 1792, leaving Bonn never to return to it even for a visit.

CHAPTER II

THE MORNING OF LIFE

Thou, O God! who sellest us all good things at the price of labor.

—LEONARDO DA VINCI

Closely following his arrival in Vienna, Beethoven began studying composition with Haydn, applying himself with great diligence to the work in hand; but master and pupil did not get along together very well. There were many dissonances from the start. It was not in the nature of things that two beings so entirely dissimilar in their point of view should work together harmoniously. Beethoven, original, independent, iconoclastic, acknowledged no superior, without having as yet achieved anything to demonstrate his superiority; Haydn, tied down to established forms, subservient, meek, was only happy when sure of the approbation of his superiors. His attitude toward those above him in rank was characterized by respect and deference; he probably expected something similar from Beethoven toward himself. Haydn was then at the height of his fame, courted and admired by all, and his patience was sorely tried by the insolence of his fiery young pupil. He nicknamed Beethoven the Grand Mogul, and did not have much good to say of him to others. The pittance which he received for these lessons was no inducement to him, as he was in receipt of an income much beyond his requirements. The time given up to these lessons could have been better employed in composing.

Haydn and Beethoven, however, were in a measure supplementary to one another as regards the life-work of each. Haydn paved the way for Beethoven, who was his successor in the large orchestral forms. He and also Mozart were pioneers in the field which Beethoven made peculiarly his own. Haydn also directed Beethoven's attention to the study of Haendel and Bach, whose works Beethoven always held most highly in esteem. It is true that Beethoven, even in the old Bonn days, was familiar to some extent with the works of these masters; but his opportunity for getting at this kind of music was limited in Bonn. Vienna, the musical center of the world at that time, was, as may be supposed, a much better field in this respect. The study of these profound works of genius under the leadership and eulogy of so prominent a musician as Haydn had much to do with shaping Beethoven's ideals. These masters gave an example of solidity and earnestness which is characteristic of their work. Haydn and Mozart, on the other hand, appealed to him in his lighter moods, in the play of fancy, in the capricious and humorous conceits of which he has given such fine examples in the symphonies and sonatas.

The lessons to Beethoven continued for a little over a year, or until Haydn left on another visit to England in January of 1794. So eager was he for advancement, that he took lessons from another teacher at the same time, carefully concealing the fact from Haydn. Beethoven always maintained that he had not learned much from him.

Strangely, Haydn had no idea at this time or for some years

after that his pupil would ever amount to much in musical composition. He lived long enough to find Beethoven's position as a musician firmly established, but not long enough to witness his greatest triumphs.

On the departure of Haydn he began with Albrechtsberger in composition, also having violin, and even vocal lessons from other masters. Beethoven realized, on coming to Vienna, more fully than before, the necessity for close application to his studies. Though a finished performer, he knew but little of counterpoint, and the more purely scientific side of his art had been neglected. That he applied himself with all the ardor of his nature to his studies we know. They were given precedence over everything else. He even delayed for a long while writing a rondo which he had promised to Eleonore von Breuning and when he finally sent it, it was with an apology for not sending a sonata, which had also been promised.

It is characteristic of Beethoven that his teachers in general were not greatly impressed by him. We have seen how it was in the case of Haydn. Albrechtsberger was more pronounced in his disapproval. "He has learned nothing; he never will learn anything," was his verdict regarding Beethoven. This was surely small encouragement. Beethoven's original and independent way of treating musical forms brought on this censure. As he advanced in musical knowledge he took the liberty to think for himself; a very culpable proceeding with teachers of the stamp of Albrechtsberger. The young man's intuitive faculties, the surest source of all knowledge according to Schopenhauer, were developed to an abnormal degree. By the aid of this inner light he was able to see truer and farther than his pedantic old master, with the result that the pupil would argue out questions with him on subjects connected with his lessons which subverted all discipline, and well-nigh reversed their relative positions. Beethoven's audacity—his self-confidence, is brought out still more strongly when we reflect on the distinguished position held by Albrechtsberger, both as teacher and composer. He was director of music at St. Stephen's and was in great demand as a teacher. Some of his pupils became distinguished musicians, among them Huemmel, Seyfried and Weigl. He excelled in counterpoint, and was a prolific composer, although his works are but little known at the present day. He was set in his ways, a strict disciplinarian, conservative to the backbone, and upward of sixty years of age. We can readily believe there were stormy times during these lessons. There is no doubt however, that Beethoven learned a great deal from him, as is evident from the exercises still in existence from this period, embracing the various forms of fugue and counterpoint, simple, double, and triple, canon and imitation. He was thorough in his teaching and Beethoven was eager to learn, so they had at least one point in common, and the pupil made rapid headway. But his originality and fertility in ideas, which showed itself at times in a disregard for established forms when his genius was hampered thereby—qualities which even in Albrechtsberger's lifetime were to place his pupil on a pinnacle above all other composers of the period, were neither understood nor approved by the teacher. Under the circumstances, it is not surprising that the lessons continued but little over a year. His studies in theory and composition seem to have come to an end with Albrechtsberger; we hear of no other teacher having been engaged thereafter.

Shortly after Beethoven came to Vienna, his father died, and soon after the two brothers Johann and Caspar, having no ties to keep them in Bonn, followed the elder brother, who kept a fatherly watch over them. They gave him no end of trouble for the rest of his life, but Beethoven bore the burden willingly and was sincerely attached to them. All the honor and nobility of the family seems to have centered in him.

On his arrival in Vienna he carried letters of introduction from Count Waldstein and from the Elector, which opened to him the doors of the best houses. His intrinsic worth did the rest. One of his earliest Vienna friends was Prince Lichnowsky, a person who seems to have possessed a combination of all those noble qualities that go to make up the character of a gentleman. Highly cultivated and enthusiastic on the subject of music, he had the penetration to see that in Beethoven he had before him one of the elect of all time. The Prince had been a pupil of Mozart and an ardent admirer of the deceased master. Providentially, Beethoven appeared on the scene soon after Mozart's decease, and received the devotion and admiration that had formerly been given Mozart. In this he was ably seconded by his wife, who shared with him the admiration and reverential wonder which such highly endowed people would be apt to accord to a man of genius. One of the first acts of this princely couple was to give Beethoven a pension of 600 florins per year. This was but the beginning of unexampled kindness on their part. They followed this by giving him a home in their residence on the Schotten bastion, and we find him well launched in the social life of the gayest capital in Europe.

This practical help was invaluable to Beethoven, for with the aid which he had from the Elector, it was almost enough to assure him independence. It not only increased his opportunities for study, but, his mind being free from care, he was enabled to profit more by his studies. The Lichnowskys were older than Beethoven and were childless. He was allowed to do as he pleased; a privilege of which he availed himself without hesitation. They entertained considerably and their social position was unexceptionable. They maintained a small orchestra for the performance of the music he liked and for his own compositions. He was always the honored guest, and met the best people of Vienna. The devotion of the Princess, in particular, was always in evidence.

It can be readily understood that with such an original character as Beethoven, headstrong and impatient of restraint, a pleasant smooth life was not to be expected. The arrangement would seem to have been an excellent one for him, but he did not so regard it. Already at odds with the world, misunderstanding people and being misunderstood, he soon came to realize that a life of solitude was the only resource for a man constituted as he was. He never considered himself under any obligation to the Prince, or rather, he acted as though he felt the obligation to be the other way. He acted independently from the start, taking his meals at a restaurant whenever it suited his convenience, and showing an ungovernable temper when interfered with in any way. But the kindness and patience of the Princess never failed her; after any trouble it was she who smoothed the difficulty and restored harmony. She was like an indulgent mother to him; in her eyes he could do no wrong.

Prince Lichnowsky was wholly unaccustomed to this sort of thing. It is certain that he never met with anything of the kind from Mozart, and there were times when his patience was sorely tried by Beethoven. The Princess, with a sweetness and graciousness which Beethoven appreciated, always made peace between them. He afterward said that her solicitude was carried to such a length that she wished to put him under a glass shade, "that no unworthy person might touch or breathe on me."

Of course this kind of thing only confirmed the young man in his course. It was kindness, but it was not wisdom. Few people are so constituted as to be able to stand praise and adulation without the character suffering thereby. Censure would have been much better for him. When the individual is attacked, when he is made to assume the defensive, he first discovers the vulnerable points in his armor, and as opportunity offers strengthens them. Beethoven's ungovernable

George Alexander Fischer

temper and apparent ingratitude are frequently commented on, but the ingratitude was only apparent. When he came to a knowledge of himself and discovered that he was in the wrong in any controversy or quarrel, and it must be admitted they were frequent enough all through his life, he would make amends for it so earnestly, with such vehement self-denunciation, and show such contrition, that it would be impossible for any of his friends to hold out against him. Then there would be a short love-feast, during which the offended party would possibly be the recipient of a dedication from the master, and things would go on smoothly until the next break. The Prince soon learned to make all sorts of concessions to his headstrong guest, and even went so far as to order his servant to give Beethoven the precedence, in case he and Beethoven were to ring at the same time.

But Beethoven did not like the new life. Even the little restraint that it imposed was irksome to him, and the arrangement came to an end in about two years. But the friendship continued for many years. Beethoven's opus 1 is dedicated to the Prince, as well as the grand Sonata Pathetique, and the Second Symphony, also the opus 179, consisting of nine variations, and the grand Sonata in A Flat. To the Princess Lichnowsky he dedicated opus 157, variations on "See the Conquering Hero Comes." He also dedicated several of his compositions to Count Moritz Lichnowsky, a younger brother of the Prince.

Among the other friends of this period may be mentioned Prince Lobkowitz, who was an ardent admirer of Beethoven, Prince Kinski, and also Count Browne to whose wife Beethoven dedicated the set of Russian variations. In acknowledgment of this honor, the Count presented Beethoven with a horse. He accepted it thankfully and then forgot all about it until some months after, when a large bill came in for its keep. There was also Count Brunswick and the Baron von Swieten, and most of the music-loving aristocracy of Vienna, who it appears could not see enough of him. His music and his individuality charmed them and he was beset with invitations. Baron von Swieten was one of his earliest and staunchest friends. His love and devotion to music knew no bounds. He gave concerts at his residence with a full band, and produced music of the highest order, Haendel and Sebastian Bach being his favorites, the music being interpreted in the best manner. It is related that the old Baron would keep Beethoven after the others had left, making him play far into the night and would sometimes put him up at his own house so that he might keep him a little longer. A note from the Baron to Beethoven is preserved, in which he says, "If you can call next Wednesday I shall be glad to see you. Come at half-past eight in the evening with your nightcap in your pocket."

These social successes, however, did not lead to idleness. He kept up the practise all his life of recording his musical thoughts in sketch-books, which latter are an object lesson to those engaged in creative work as showing the extraordinary industry of the man and his absorption in his work. Many of these are preserved in the different museums, those in the British Museum being a notable collection. Some of the work of this period was afterwards utilized by being incorporated into the work of his riper years.

Beethoven's talents as a performer were freely acknowledged by all with whom he came in contact. When we come to the question of his creative talent, we can only marvel at the slowness with which his powers unfolded themselves. His opus 1 appeared in 1795, when he was twenty-four years old. There was nothing of the prodigy about him in composition. At twenty-four, Mozart had achieved some of his greatest triumphs.

Beethoven's work however, shows intellectuality of the highest kind, and this, whether in music or literature, is not produced easily or spontaneously; it is of slow growth, the product of a ripened mind, attained only by infinite labor and constant striving after perfection, with the highest ideals before one.

He had been trying his hand at composition for many years, but was always up to this time known as a performer rather than as a composer, although he frequently played his own compositions, and had as we have seen, great talent at improvising, which in itself is a species of composition, and an indication of musical abilities of the highest order.

All the great masters of music delighted in the exercise of this talent, although it is now rarely attempted in public, Chopin having been one of the last to exercise it. Bach excelled in it, sometimes developing themes in the form of a fugue at a public performance. No preparation would be possible under these circumstances, as in many cases the theme would be given by one of the audience.

This art of improvising, as these masters practised it,—who can explain it or tell how it is done? All we know is that the brain conceives the thought, and on the instant the fingers execute it in ready obedience to the impulse sent out by the brain, the result being a finished performance, not only so far as the melody is concerned, but in harmony and counterpoint as well. Mozart, at the age of fourteen, at Mantua, on his second Italian tour, improvised a sonata and fugue at a public concert, taking the impressionable Italians by storm, and such performances he repeated frequently in after years. Beethoven excelled in this direction as greatly as he after-ward did in composition, towering high over his contem-poraries. Czerny, pupil of Beethoven and afterward teacher of Liszt, states that Beethoven's improvisations created the greatest sensation during the first few years of his stay in Vienna. The theme was sometimes original, some-times given by the auditors. In Allegro movements there would be bravura passages, often more difficult than anything in his published works. Sometimes it would be in the form of variations after the manner of his Choral Fantasia, op. 80, or the last movement of the Choral Symphony. All authorities agree as to Beethoven's genius in improvising. His playing was better under these circum-stances than when playing a written composition, even when it was written by himself.

Once Huemmel undertook a contest with Beethoven in improvising. After he had been playing for some time Beethoven interrupted him with the question, "When are you going to begin?" It is needless to say that Beethoven, when his turn came to play, distanced the other so entirely that there was no room for comparison.

CHAPTER III

THE NEW PATH

I tremble to the depths of my soul and ask my daemon: "Why this cup to me?"

—WAGNER

Life at last has found a meaning.

—WAGNER: *Letter to Frau Wille*

Reference has already been made to the fact that Beethoven's opus 1 was published in 1795, something like three years after taking up his residence in Vienna, and when he was twenty-four years of age. It consists of three Trios for piano and strings. When Haydn returned from London and heard these Trios, the master criticised one of them and advised him not to publish it. Beethoven thought this particular one the best of the three, and others concur with him in this opinion. Shortly after, he published his opus 2, consisting of three sonatas dedicated to Haydn, besides variations and smaller pieces. But this does not by any means give the amount of his compositions for this period, some of which were not published until many years afterward.

All this time, Beethoven, though playing frequently at the houses of his aristocratic friends, had not yet made his appearance in public, but about the time that his opus 1 appeared, he played at a concert given in aid of the Widow's Fund of the Artists' Society. He composed for this occasion a Grand Concerto (opus 15) in C major for piano and orchestra, taking the piano part himself. It was finished on the day preceding that on which the concert was held, the copyists waiting in another room for their parts. At the rehearsal, the piano being one-half note out of tune, he transposed it into C sharp, playing it without the notes. Very soon after, he appeared again in public, at a concert given for the benefit of Mozart's widow, when he played one of Mozart's concertos. The beginning once made, he appeared rather frequently as a performer, not only in Vienna, but extended his trips the next year as far as Berlin, where he encountered Huemmel.

But Beethoven's mind was always turned toward composition. It had been the aim of his life, even at Bonn, to become a great creative artist. For this he had left his native city, and the larger opportunities for musical culture afforded by his life in Vienna must have directed his thoughts still more strongly into this channel. An important social event of the period was the annual ball of the Artists' Society of Vienna. Suesmayer, pupil and intimate friend of Mozart, the composer of several of the "Mozart Masses," had composed music for this ball and Beethoven was asked to contribute something likewise, with the result that he composed twelve waltzes and twelve minuets for it. He also had in hand at the same time piano music, songs, and studies in orchestral composition. Nothing which he produced in these years, however, gave any forecast of what he would eventually attain to. This is paralleled in the case of Bach, who, up to his thirtieth year was more famous as a performer than as composer.

Beethoven's earlier compositions were regarded as the clever product of an ambitious young musician. Although later in life, he all but repudiated the published work of these years, some of the thoughts from the sketch-books of this period were utilized in the work of his best years.

He acquired a habit early in life of carrying a note-book when away from his rooms, in which he recorded musical ideas as they came to him. His brain teemed with them; these he entered indiscriminately, good and bad, assorting them later, discarding some, altering others, seldom retaining a musical thought exactly as it was first presented to his consciousness. Music became the one absorbing passion of his life. It took the place of wife and children; it was of more importance to him than home or any other consideration. His compositions show continual progress toward artistic perfection to the end of his life, and this was attained only by infinite labor.

It may not be out of place here to reflect on the essentially unselfish character of the man of genius. He lives and strives, not for himself, but for others; he pursues an objective end only. Among the forces making for the regeneration of mankind, he is foremost.

There is little of importance to record concerning Beethoven for the few years following the publication of his opus 1. He continued to perform occasionally in public, and also gave a few lessons, but his time was taken up with study and composition for the most part. It was a period of earnest endeavor, the compositions of which consist of the better class of piano music, as well as trios, quartets and occasional songs, his work being much in the style of Mozart and Haydn; the quality of emotional power and intellectuality not yet having appeared to any extent.

His great productions, those that show his genius well developed, are coincident with the beginning of the nineteenth century. The years 1800 and 1801 were an epoch with him as a composer. He was now thirty, and was beginning to show of what stuff he was made. These two years saw the production of some of the imperishable works of the master, namely: the First Symphony, the Oratorio *Christus am Oelberg*, and the Prometheus Ballet Music. It is probable that he had given earnest thought to these works for some years previously, and had had them in hand for two years or more before their appearance. The First Symphony calls for special mention as in it the future Symphonist is already foreshadowed. He was almost a beginner at orchestral work, but it marks an epoch in this class of composition, raising it far beyond anything of the kind that had yet appeared. Viewed in the light of later ones it is apparent that he held himself in; that he was tentative compared with his subsequent ones. Considered as a symphony and compared with what had been produced in this class up to that time, it is a daring innovation and was regarded as such by the critics. He broadened and enlarged the form and gave it a dignity that was unknown to it before this time.

Beethoven's sonatas are as superior to those that had preceded them as are his symphonies. He enlarged them, developed the Scherzo from the Minuet and made them of more importance in every way. With Haydn the Minuet was gay and lively, a style of music well adapted to Haydn's particular temperament and character; but Beethoven in the Scherzo carried the idea further than anything of which Haydn had dreamed. Before Beethoven's First Symphony appeared, he had composed a dozen or more sonatas and was in a position to profit by the experience gained thereby. He felt his way in these, the innovations all turning out to be improvements.

George Alexander Fischer

One has only to compare the sonatas of Mozart and Haydn with those of Beethoven to be at once impressed with the enormous importance of the latter. As has been stated, the experience gained with the sonata was utilized in the First Symphony, each succeeding one showing growth. Beethoven's artistic instinct was correct, but he did not trust to this alone. He proceeded carefully, weighing the matter well, and his judgment was usually right. There is evidence from his exercise books that he had this Symphony in mind as early as 1795. It was first produced on April 2, 1800, at a concert which he gave for his own benefit at the Burg theatre. On this occasion he improvised on the theme of the Austrian National Hymn, recently composed by Haydn, well known in this country through its insertion in the Hymnal of the Protestant Episcopal Church, under the title of Austria. Beethoven's hearing was sufficiently intact at this time to enable him to hear his symphonies performed, an important matter while his judgment was being formed.

The Prometheus Ballet Music, opus 43, consisting of overture, introduction and sixteen numbers, was first performed early in 1801, and achieved immediate success, so much so that it was published at once as pianoforte music. In addition to the Prometheus, there is to be credited to this period the C minor concerto, opus 37, a septet for strings and wind, opus 20, a number of quartets, and other compositions. The *Christus am Oelberg* (The Mount of Olives), opus 85, Beethoven's first great choral work, has already been mentioned. In this oratorio Jesus appears as one of the characters, for which he has been severely criticised. His judgment was at fault in another respect also in having the concert stage too much in mind. The composition at times is operatic in character, while the text calls for a mode of treatment solemn and religious, as in Passion-music. If set to some other text, this work would be well nigh faultless; the recitatives are singularly good, and there is a rich orchestration. It is reminiscent of Haendel and prophetic of Wagner. The Hallelujah Chorus in particular is a magnificent piece of work. As is the case with the Messiah, its beauties as well as its defects are so apparent, so pronounced, that the latter serve as a foil to bring out its good qualities in the strongest relief. It was first performed in the spring of 1803, in Vienna, on which occasion Beethoven played some of his other compositions. It was repeated three times within the year.

Other contributions of 1801 are two grand sonatas, the "Pastorale" in D, opus 28, the Andante of which is said to have been a favorite of Beethoven's and was often played by him, and the one in A flat, opus 26, dedicated to Prince Karl Lichnowsky and containing a grand funeral march. Then there are the sonatas in E flat and C sharp minor, published together as opus 27, and designated Quasi una Fantasia. The latter is famous as the "Moonlight" sonata, dedicated to Julia Guicciardi. Neither of these names were authorized by Beethoven. Besides these, there are the two violin sonatas, A minor, and F, dedicated to Count Fries, and lesser compositions. The Second Symphony (in D) is the chief production of 1802. In addition there are the two piano sonatas in G, and D minor, opus 31, and three sonatas for violin and piano, opus 30, the latter dedicated to the Emperor of Russia. They form a striking example of Beethoven's originality and the force of his genius, and must have been caviar to his public.

The Second Symphony is a great advance on the first, and consequently a greater departure from the advice laid down to him by others. His independence and absolute faith in himself and the soundness of his judgment are clearly illustrated here. The composition is genial and in marked contrast to the gloomy forebodings that filled his mind at this time. The second movement, the Larghetto, is interesting on account of the introduction of conversation among the groups of instruments, an innovation which he exploited to a much greater extent in subsequent works. In the Larghetto one group occasionally interrupts the other, giving it piquancy. There is a rhythm and swing to it which makes it the most enjoyable of the four movements. The critics hacked it again as might have been expected, the result being that the next one diverged still more from their idea of what a good symphony should be.

It was at this period that life's tragedy began to press down on him. He had left youth behind, and had entered on a glorious manhood. He was the idol of his friends, although his fame as a great composer had yet to be established. The affirmations of his genius were plainly apparent to him, if not to others, and he knew that he was on the threshold of creating imperishable masterpieces. A great future was opening out before him, which, however, was in great part to be nullified by his approaching deafness and other physical ailments. His letters at this time to his friend Dr. Wegeler, at Bonn, and to others, are full of misgivings.

But not alone is this unhappy frame of mind to be attributed to approaching deafness or any mere physical ailment. The psychological element also enters into the account and largely dominates it. The extraordinary character of the First and Second Symphonies seem to have had a powerful effect on his trend of thought making him introspective and morbidly conscientious. In a mind constituted as was his, it is quite within bounds to assume that the revelation of his genius was largely the cause of the morbid self-consciousness which appears in his letters of the period, and in the "Will." He recognized to the full how greatly superior this work was to anything of the kind that had yet appeared; singularly the knowledge made him humble. What he had accomplished thus far was only an earnest of the great work he was capable of, but to achieve it meant a surrender of nearly all the ties that bound him to life. The human qualities in him rebelled at the prospect. With the clairvoyance superinduced by much self-examination, he was able to forecast the vast scope of his powers, and the task that was set him. The whole future of the unapproachable artist that he was destined to become, was mirrored out to him almost at the beginning of his career, but he saw it only with apprehension and dread. There were periods when a narrower destiny would have pleased him more. "Unto whomsoever much is given, of him shall much be required." He at times recoiled from the task, and would have preferred death instead. This was probably the most unhappy period of his life. He had yet to learn the hardest lesson of all, resignation, renunciation. That harsh mandate enunciated by Goethe in Faust: "Entbaeren sollst du, sollst entbaeren," had been thrust on him with a force not to be gainsaid or evaded.

With such a man but one issue to the conflict was possible: obedience to the higher law. In a conversation held with his friend Krumpholz, he expressed doubts as to the value of his work hitherto. "From now on I shall strike out on a new road," he said. He is now dominated by a greater seriousness; his mission has been shown him. Adieu now to the light-hearted mode of life characteristic of his friends and of the time. His new road led him into regions where they could not follow; from now on he was more and more unlike his fellows, more misunderstood, isolated, a prophet in the wilderness. Placed here by Providence specially for a unique work, he at first does not seem to have understood it in this light, and reached out, the spirit of the man, after happiness, occasional glimpses of which came to him, as it does to all sooner or later. He soon found, however, that happiness was not intended for him, or rather, that he was not intended for it. Something higher and better he could have, but not this. On coming to Vienna, and while living with Prince Lichnowsky, he made so much of a concession to public opinion as to buy a court suit, and he even took dancing lessons, but he never learned dancing, never even learned how to wear the court suit properly, and soon gave up both in disgust. The principle on which he now conducted his life was to give his genius full play, to obey its every mandate, to allow no obstacle to come in the way of its fullest development. That this idea controlled him throughout life, is apparent in many ways, but most of all in his journal. "Make once more the sacrifice of all the petty necessities of life for the glory of thy art. God before all," he wrote in 1818, when beginning the Mass in D. All sorts of circumstances and influences were required to isolate him from the world to enable him the better to do his appointed work. Probably no other musician ever made so complete a surrender of all impedimenta for the sake of his art as did Beethoven.

Music as an art does not conduce to renunciation, since its outward expression always partakes more or less of the nature of a festival. The claims of society come more insistently into the life of the musician than in that of other art-workers, the painter or literary man, for instance, whose work is completed in the isolation of his study. The musician, on the contrary, completes his work on the stage. He must participate in its rendering. He is, more than any other, beset by social obligations; he perforce becomes to a certain extent gregarious, all of which has a tendency to dissipate time and energy. It is only by a great effort that he can isolate himself; that he can retain his individuality. Beethoven's reward on these lines was great in proportion to his victory over himself.

CHAPTER IV

HEROIC SYMPHONY

Ach, der menschliche Intellekt! Ach "Genie"! Es ist nicht so gar viel einen "Faust" eine Schopenhauerische Philosophie, eine Eroika gemacht zu haben.

—FRIEDERICH NIETZSHE

The immediate fruit of this mental travail was a sudden growth or expansion of his creative powers. This is apparent in his work, marking the beginning of the second period. His compositions now suggest thought. There is a fecundating power in them which generates thought, and it is in the moral nature that this force is most apparent. His work now begins to be a vital part of himself, the spiritual essence, communicating to his followers somewhat of his own strength and force of character. Once having entered on the new path, he reached, in the Third Symphony, the pinnacle of greatness almost at a bound. He was now, at thirty-four, at the height of his colossal powers. His titanic genius in its swift development showed an ability almost preternatural. One immortal work of genius succeeded another with marvelous rapidity.

George Alexander Fischer

The Third Symphony calls for more than passing notice. Beethoven's altruism is well known. The brotherhood of man was a favorite theme with him. By the aid of his mighty intellect and his intuitional powers, he saw more clearly than others the world's great need. The inequalities in social conditions were more clearly marked in those times than now. The French Revolution had set people thinking. Liberty and equality was what they were demanding. Beethoven personally had nothing to gain and everything to risk by siding with the people. All his personal friends were of the aristocracy. It was this class which fostered the arts, music in particular. From the time that Beethoven came to Vienna as a young man, up to the end of his life, he enjoyed one or more pensions given him by members of the upper classes. But his sympathies were with the people. By honoring Napoleon with the dedication of the Third Symphony, he would have antagonized the Imperial family, and perhaps many of the aristocracy, but this phase of the question may not have occurred to him, and if it had, it would not have deterred him.

Beethoven's attitude toward Napoleon could have had no other construction placed upon it than that of strong partisanship, since there was no artistic bond to unite them. The arch-enemy of Imperialism, as he was considered at this time, the mightiest efforts of the young Corsican had hitherto been directed specially against Austria. Beethoven did not approve of war; he expressed himself plainly on this point in after years, but at this period considered it justifiable and necessary as a means of abolishing what remained of feudal authority.

Austria had been the first to feel the iron hand of Napoleon. His first important military achievement, and what is generally conceded to be the greatest in his entire military career, was his campaign against the Austrians in Italy, which took place in the spring of 1796, shortly after his marriage. His victories over them first gave him fame, not only in France, but throughout Europe. Within a month from the time that he took command in the Italian campaign, he won six victories over them, giving the French army the command of the whole range of the Alps. Within a year he had driven the Austrians out of Italy, many thousands of prisoners were taken, ten thousand men had been killed or wounded, fifty-five pieces of cannon had been taken, besides rich provinces, which he looted to enrich France. He pursued his campaign into Austria, getting to within ninety miles of Vienna with his army, where he dictated terms of peace to the Emperor, which were highly advantageous to France. Appalled by these catastrophies, the court was even preparing to flee from Vienna and was arranging for the safe carriage of the treasure, when the Emperor accepted Napoleon's terms. The humiliation to Austria was accentuated by the fact that her armies were nearly twice that of France. They were also in good condition, while the French armies were ragged and half starved. With this inferior equipment Bonaparte humbled the most haughty nation in Europe in the space of a year. He defeated them again in 1800, at Marengo, and was at all times their arch-enemy.

All this happened some years before the period of which we are writing. Beethoven regarded Napoleon as a liberator, a savior, on account of his success in restoring order out of chaos in France. It showed considerable moral courage on his part to come out so plainly for Napoleon. A broader question than patriotism, however, was here involved. Patriotism seeks the good of a small section. Altruism embraces the good of all, thus including patriotism.

The idea of writing the symphony to Napoleon may have been suggested to Beethoven by General Bernadotte, who was then the Ambassador of the French at Vienna. He and

Count Moritz Lichnowsky were intimate friends and saw a good deal of Beethoven at that time. The three young men no doubt discussed social conditions and politics, as well as music, and it would have been an easy task for the General, who had served under Napoleon, to excite Beethoven's enthusiasm for the Liberator of France. In after years, when General Bernadotte became King of Sweden, he still retained his interest in the events of this period.

This Symphony was the best work which Beethoven had yet accomplished; a work the grandeur and sublimity of which must have been a surprise to himself. It was conceived in the spirit of altruism, to show his appreciation of the man whom he believed was destined more than any other to uplift humanity. In the quality of its emotional expression, and also in its dimensions, it far exceeded anything of the kind that had yet appeared. Beethoven himself advised, on account of its great length, that it be placed at the beginning of a program rather than at its end. It is unique as a symphony, just as Napoleon was unique as a man. On finishing the work he put the name of Bonaparte on the title-page.

BONAPARTE

LUDWIG VAN BEETHOVEN.

With perfect propriety the concept is here established that two great men are before the world, Napoleon and Beethoven, and that the latter is as great in his own province as was Napoleon in his, each being the exponent of a new order of things, co-equal in the achievement of great deeds. Posterity, in exalting the one and debasing the other, shows how modest Beethoven was in the matter.

He was on the point of sending it to Paris when the news was brought him by his pupil Ries, that Napoleon was declared

Emperor. In a rage Beethoven tore off the title-page containing the dedication, and threw it to the floor. "The man will become a tyrant and will trample all human rights under foot. He is no more than an ordinary man!" was Beethoven's exclamation. He finally gave it the name of Sinfonia Eroica, in memory of a great man. It is dedicated to Prince Lobkowitz, who had it performed before Prince Louis Ferdinand. The Prince was greatly taken with it, at once recognizing its worth and insisting on hearing it three times in succession the same evening.

This year saw the production of two of Beethoven's most famous pianoforte sonatas, the Waldstein, already referred to in this work, dedicated to the friend of his youth, Count Waldstein, and the Appassionata, dedicated to Count von Brunswick, sublime conceptions that glow with the fire of genius.

Mention must also be made of the famous Kreutzer Sonata, opus 47, for piano and violin, which was completed prior to the Third Symphony. This great work was originally intended for an English violinist resident at Vienna by the name of Bridgetower, and was first performed at a morning concert at the Augarten in May of 1803. Beethoven was at the piano and Bridgetower played the violin part. Beethoven had completed a portion of the work the previous year, but the violin part had to be played almost before the ink was dry, the piano accompaniment being made up by Beethoven as he went along. Notwithstanding this entire want of preparation, the value of the work was so apparent that it produced an encore.

Beethoven changed his mind about the dedication, and a year or two later this distinction was conferred on a friend, Rudolph Kreutzer, violinist and composer, who had come to Vienna in 1798 with Bernadotte, and as a matter of course, became acquainted with Beethoven. Kreutzer had been a protege of Marie Antoinette; afterward he was taken up by Napoleon, and still later by Louis XVIII, each of whom he served in his musical capacity. The Kreutzer Sonata has had a wide notoriety given it through Tolstoy's work of that name.

CHAPTER V

FIDELIO

In the mind as in a field, some things may be sown and carefully brought up, yet that which springs naturally is most pleasing.

—TACITUS

The year 1805 saw Beethoven hard at work in a field new to him,—operatic composition. It had probably been in his mind for some years to write an opera. In those days almost every composer wrote operas, and to have written a successful one carried with it, not only a certain prestige, but substantial rewards in a financial sense. Outside of the church but little opportunity was afforded the general public to gratify its love for music other than in opera. Orchestral concerts were comparatively rare,—song recitals unknown. The development of the orchestra was just beginning, through the genius of Beethoven, and the Viennese were to a great extent, still unconscious of its importance, as a means of musical expression. The many symphonies, quartets, and other forms of chamber-music of Haydn, Mozart and contemporaneous composers, were for the most part written for private performance at musical functions in the houses of the nobility, or for friends of the composers.

Beethoven believed that if he were to write one or two operas, his income would be reinforced to such an extent as to enable him to give his attention wholly to the production of symphonies and masses, a style of composition to which he was inclined by temperament. In the early symphonies we already have a foreshadowing of what he could do in the production of great orchestral music, the desire for which in later years controlled him wholly. Like most men of genius Beethoven had little regard for money, and until middle age was reached, never thought of saving any. He valued it only in so far as he could use it for himself or others. It may be said in passing that he gave it away freely, glad to be of service to others. His income, augmented by his copyrights, did not keep pace with his expenditures; when a friend needed money and he had none, he would give him a composition instead, which the other would turn into cash.

The manager of the theatre, An der Wien, had, before this, made overtures to Beethoven to write an opera, and he went so far as to take up his quarters in the theatre, preparatory to this work; but a change in the management made it necessary to give up the idea for the time being. In 1804, the offer in regard to the opera was renewed, and work was begun upon it. It took up a large part of his time until its production in November of 1805. It is probable that he took more pains with this work than was devoted to any other of his compositions with the exception of the Mass in D. His capacity for work was extraordinary, particularly at this time, and the delight that he experienced in producing these masterpieces was still new to him, which in itself was an incentive to great exertion. His approaching deafness also had a good deal to do with his great activity. The ailment had progressed steadily from the time of its first appearance; at the time of which we write he had abandoned all hope of any aid from medical treatment; by throwing himself heart and soul into his work, he could forget for the time the misfortune which was closing in on him. He feared that a period of absolute deafness might set in when he would be unable to hear any of his works, and the desire must have been great to accomplish as much as possible before that time should come.

Beethoven does not seem to have been very hard to suit in the way of a libretto at this time. He probably gave the matter very little consideration except on one point,—its morality. His high ideals, and his innate purity of mind, caused him to dislike and condemn the sort of story which was usually worked up into operatic libretti in those days, in which intrigue and illicit love formed the staple material. He expressed himself strongly on this subject, even criticising Mozart for having set Don Giovanni to music, saying that it degraded the art. So strongly did he feel about it that he seems to have thought almost any libretto would do, provided the moral sentiment contained in it were sufficiently prominent. Later, the experience which he gained with Fidelio showed him that the libretto of an opera is indeed a very important matter; then he went to the other extreme, and was unable to find anything which would satisfy him, although many libretti were submitted to him at various times during the remainder of his life. A quantity of them were found among his papers after his death. Bouilly's libretto Leonore, which had been set to music by two different composers before Beethoven took it in hand, was finally selected, and Sonnleithner was employed to translate it from the French. The name of the opera was changed to Fidelio, but the various overtures written for it are still known as the Leonore overtures.

Beethoven took up his quarters in the theatre again as soon as the libretto was ready for him and went to work at it with a will. But he was not at his best in operatic writing,—this symphonist, this creator of great orchestral forms. The opera was an alien soil to him; composition—never an easy matter to Beethoven, was more difficult than ever in the case of Fidelio. The sketch-books show the many attempts and alterations in the work, at its every stage. In addition, he was handicapped at the outset by an unsuitable libretto. The Spanish background, for one thing, was a clog, as his trend of thought and sympathies were thoroughly German. But this is a slight matter compared with the forbidding nature of the drama itself, with its prison scenes, its dungeons and general atmosphere of gloom. One dreary scene after another is unfolded, and the action never reaches the dignity of tragedy nor the depth of pathos which should be awakened by the portrayal of suffering. We are unable to feel that the two principal characters are martyrs; as one tiresome scene succeeds another, we come to care nothing whatever about them and are unable to sympathize with them in their suffering or rejoice in their deliverance. The first requisite in opera, it would appear, is that it be pervaded by an atmosphere of romanticism. Other things are necessary; the libretto must have dramatic situations; but above all, the romantic element must prevail. If it is difficult for the listener to become interested in an opera with such a libretto as is Fidelio, it must be doubly so for the composer who undertakes the task of writing music for it. A dull story hinders the play of fancy; the imagination remains dormant, and the product under such conditions has the air of being forced. The musician is in bonds.

Musically, it is a work of surpassing beauty; but there is a dissonance between music and libretto which gives the impression of something lacking; there is not the harmony which we expect in a work of this kind. Wagner has taught us better on these points. The music of Fidelio has force and grandeur; some of it has a sensuous beauty that reminds us of

Mozart at his best. Had Beethoven's choice fallen to a better libretto, the result might have been an altogether better opera.

Fidelio affords a good instance of the fact that operatic composition, considered strictly as music, is not the highest form in which the art can be portrayed, and that, in itself, it is not so strictly confined to the domain of music as is the symphony, or the various forms of sacred music (the oratorio or the mass, for instance). It may, in the right hands, come to be a greater work of art, viewed in its entirety, than either of the forms just mentioned. In the hands of a man like Wagner, it undoubtedly is, but in such a case the result is achieved by means other than those obtained through the domain of music. Much is contributed by the literary quality of the libretto, its poetic and romantic qualities, its dramatic possibilities, as well as its stage setting and the ability of the singers to act well their parts. An opera is a combination of several arts, in which music is often subordinated. Not so in the case of sacred music, in which the entire portrayal rests absolutely on the musician's art. Of the works of the great composers who wrote both classes of music, those which are devoted to religious subjects will be found vastly superior in almost every instance, with the one exception of Mozart's and in the case of this composer, his Mass in B flat and the Requiem will bear comparison with any of his operas. With no regular income, Mozart was compelled to write operas in order to live, but his preference was for sacred music. Haydn, on the other hand, spent no time on grand opera. Through his connection with the Princes Esterhazy, which gave him an assured income from his twenty-ninth year to the end of his life, he was in a position to write only the style of music to which he was best adapted by his talents and preference.

Above all other considerations, the opera must be made to pay. The composers expected to make money from it, and its presentation was always accompanied by enormous expense. Everything conspired to get them to write what their audience would like, without considering too closely whether this was the best they were capable of producing. In those times all that people required of an opera was that it should entertain. If we compare the best opera before Wagner's time with such works as Bach's Grand Mass in B minor, or Beethoven's Mass in D, we will readily see that the composers of those times put their best thought into their sacred compositions. Bach, Protestant that he was, but with the vein of religious mysticism strong in him, which is usually to be found in highly endowed artistic natures (Wagner is an instance, also Liszt), was attracted by the beautiful text of the Mass, its stateliness and solemnity, and the world is enriched by an imperishable work of genius. It is significant that he wrote no opera, and Beethoven only one. Both composers probably regarded the opera as being less important artistically than the other great forms in which music is embodied.

In operatic composition, as we have seen, the musicians of those times were too apt to write down to their public. No such temptation came to them in their religious works, as no income was expected from this source. Here the composer could be independent of his public, so this branch of the art was developed to a much greater degree than the other. A high standard was thus reached and maintained in religious music.

Beethoven by temperament was not adapted to operatic composition. He was too much the philosopher, his aims being higher than were desired by an operatic audience of that time. He could best express himself in orchestral music, and his genius drew him irresistibly in this direction. This predilection appears throughout his works. In his purely orchestral compositions, his genius has absolute freedom.

When he came to opera he found himself constantly hampered by new and untried conditions. He soon found that opera has to do with something besides music. Having once begun, however, he carried it through, perforce, by almost superhuman efforts.

Wagner, poet that he was, builded better. He had the temperament for opera. He was adapted to operatic composition as if he had been specially created for the purpose. Here was the union of the poet and the musician in the same individual. Knowing the importance of the drama, and aided by his literary instinct, he was able to select interesting subjects which were well adapted to musical treatment. It was the spirit of romanticism pervading these dramas of Wagner's which enabled him to weave such music about them. We cannot imagine him making good music to a poor libretto,—with Wagner the libretto and the music were of equal importance, the two usually having been produced simultaneously; his music fits the words so well that no other would be desired.

Early in the summer, Beethoven left his quarters in the theatre and went into the country nearby, where he could work with more freedom than in the city. No labor seems to have been too great for him in the composition of this work. The opera was finished early in the fall of 1805, and as soon as he returned to town he began with the rehearsals. Then he had almost as much work as in writing the opera, everything possible having been done to worry him. His simplicity and want of tact seem to have been very much in evidence at this time; he was like a child compared with the astute men of affairs with whom he now came in contact. His greatest difficulty, however, was with his singers. A man following so faithfully the intimations of his genius as did Beethoven, withal a man of such striking individuality and force of character, would be sure to disregard to some extent the capacity of his performers. His singers made no end of trouble, stating that their parts were unsingable and asking for alterations. Some of the members of the orchestra also complained about technical difficulties, but the master was obdurate, refusing to make any changes. Instead of placating them, by which means only, a good performance was possible as things went at that time, he overrode their wishes and would make no concessions whether in large or in small matters. To Beethoven, music as an art was the most serious fact in his existence; to the others, it was no more than a means of enjoyment or of subsistence. His point of view being so different from that of the others, it is not surprising that he was always at odds with them. Trifles often annoyed him more than gross derelictions. At one of the rehearsals the third bassoon player was absent and Beethoven was enraged. That anything short of illness or disaster should keep this man from his post was a piece of insolence, an insult to the art. Prince Lobkowitz was present, and in the effort to pacify him, made light of the affair; he told him that this man's absence did not matter much, as the first and second bassoonists were present, a line of argument that served to include the Prince in Beethoven's wrath. Hofsekretaer Mahler relates the denouement of the incident. On the way home, after the rehearsal, as he and Beethoven came in sight of the Lobkowitz Platz, Beethoven, with the delinquent third bassoonist still in his mind, could not resist crossing the Platz, and shouting into the great gateway of the palace, "Lobkowitzscher Esel" (ass of a Lobkowitz).

Meanwhile, the French army, with Napoleon at its head, was advancing on Vienna and almost at the time that the opera was ready for presentation, took possession of the city. This was on November 13, 1805. The imperial family, the members of the nobility and every one else who could do so, had left the city on the approach of the French forces, but this did not discourage Beethoven. The opera was ready and must be presented. He could not have expected much of an audience as the very people who were interested in the subject had left the city. It was actually put on the stage on November 20, the audience consisting, it appears, mainly of French officers. It is not to be supposed that such a work would appeal to them, as there was no ballet, and the melodrama, instead of containing good jokes and risque anecdotes, was simply the tale of a wife's devotion. No doubt the intendant of the theatre, as well as Beethoven and the whole company were anathematized freely. It was continued for three nights and then withdrawn.

The work involved was enormous, both in the composition and in getting it ready for the stage. The rewards during Beethoven's lifetime were always slow. In its original form the opera was considered too long for the patience of the average audience, and also in parts too abstruse, which latter was probably its chief fault. The idea of revising it does not seem to have occurred to Beethoven, even after it was withdrawn; it required the utmost diplomacy on the part of his friends, Prince Lichnowsky in particular, to bring this about.

Beethoven had taken extraordinary pains with it up to the time of its representation. To make alterations now would be to acknowledge himself in error. The opera, however, was the most ambitious work he had yet attempted; to make it a success it was necessary that it be revised and altered considerably. With this object in view, Beethoven was invited by Prince Lichnowsky to meet some friends at his house to discuss the opera. The singers, Roeke and Meyer, who appeared in the cast, were of the party; also Stephen von Breuning and Sonnleithner. The score was studied at the piano and freely criticised. When one of the singers plainly stated that several pieces should be omitted entire and other portions shortened, Beethoven's rage knew no bounds. The conflict lasted well into the night, Beethoven at bay, with all his friends pitted against him. He defended every attack on this child of his brain, the latest product of his genius, and at first refused any compromise, but better counsels finally prevailed, aided probably by the Princess Lichnowsky, who so often assumed the part of peacemaker. Beethoven consented to some important excisions, and an entire revision of the opera. Stephen von Breuning, who was somewhat of a poet, and had considerable literary ability, was commissioned to make the desired changes in the libretto, cutting it down to two acts from three. The conference lasted until one in the morning, when, the point being gained, the Prince ordered supper to be brought in. Being Germans and musicians, they finished the night in the utmost good humor, Beethoven being the best natured of all, once his consent to the revision had been gained.

He immediately set about writing a new overture for it, and that imperishable work of genius, the Third Leonore overture appeared. Here we have an epitome of the succeeding music of the opera, foreshadowing in dramatic language, the grief and despair, and the final deliverance and joy of the principal actors of the drama. Wagner says of this work, "It is no longer an overture, but the mightiest of dramas in itself." Here Beethoven could use his accustomed freedom once more. He was back again in the familiar realm of instrumental music, and the storm and stress of recent experiences no doubt supplied some of the material which went into it. It is frequently used as a concert work.

The opera was produced the following spring in the revised form and with the new overture. The wisdom of the revision was at once apparent, but a quarrel between Beethoven and the intendant of the theatre led to its final withdrawal after two representations. It did not see the light again until 1814.

It was about this time that Beethoven first met Cherubini,

whose operas were favorites with the Vienna public. The Italian master made a stay of several months' duration in Vienna, and attended a performance of Fidelio.

CHAPTER VI

THE ETERNAL FEMININE

If that beauty of Shiraz would take my heart in hand, I would give for her dark mole Samarkand and Bokhara.

—HAFIZ

In Beethoven's time, Vienna was the gayest capital in Europe, the Paris of the world. The population was 300,000, every nationality in Europe being represented. It was cosmopolitan in the widest sense. The Germans of course predominated; then there were Hungarians, Italians, Sclavs, Sczechs, Magyars, Poles and Turks. The Italian element was particularly strong, and these southern and eastern races with their tendency toward art in any form, and the particular bias of the Italians toward music had an important influence on the Germans, modifying their seriousness.

The theatres were splendidly equipped and there were at least four large orchestras. Concerts for the general public were not common, the orchestras being required for operatic performances in private houses, which were splendidly given, as well as for state balls and other functions. The chief business of the well-to-do (and Vienna was a rich city), was to gratify a love for music. The cultivated class lived a life of elegant leisure, music being its alpha and omega. As already stated, it was an established custom with the wealthy to maintain a small orchestra, consisting of four or five pieces for the performance of chamber-music in their homes. Prince Karl Lichnowsky gave concerts every Friday evening, frequently taking a part in the orchestra. Regular weekly concerts were given by Baron von Swieten, Prince Lobkowitz, Count Rasoumowsky and many others. It is stated that at this period there were ten private theatres in Vienna, each with its complement of actors. It was a common occurrence to give operettas at these private theatres,—the ordinary parts being taken by amateurs.

How could they, we naturally ask, get an audience, when so many performances were in progress, and how could the people get around to so many places? The answer is: these performances were given daily, including Sunday, and at all hours of the day, some concerts being given as early as six o'clock in the morning. It was indeed a "golden age for Beethoven," as Schindler remarks. Thayer gives a list of twenty-one great houses open to Beethoven, nine of which belonged to princes. The young musician was often the guest of honor at the various musical functions given by these people, and received much attention from illustrious persons who were attracted to him by the force of his character as well as his genius. Not in any degree a society man, rough in exterior and careless of appearance, he was sought after by the most exclusive of Vienna society.

That a man of such force and originality, such independence, should have won the lifelong friendship of those of his own sex, goes without saying. His very scorn for the conventions and refinements of life, the manliness which was reflected in his every act, in the tones of his voice and the expression of his face, all this, united to such talents, would be sure to win the enthusiastic admiration of his fellow-men. But that the beautiful society women of the capital should have been attracted to a man so uncouth may at first sight seem surprising, until we consider that he attracted them in spite of these drawbacks and on account of other qualities, such as his sensibility, his earnestness and devotion to his art, and the wealth of his emotional and intellectual nature. He thoroughly enjoyed standing so well socially with these ladies, who in family connections were above him, but who were willing to sit at his feet in homage to his genius. Beginning with hero worship on the part of these devotees, the sentiment usually developed into the more intimate relation of friendship or love. The "Ewig Weibliche" appears constantly in his music and was always in his life. He formed many romantic attachments which may not always have been Platonic, but they were always pure. Beethoven had as chivalrous a regard for women as had any knight of the middle ages.

Among those with whom he became intimate are the Baroness Ertmann, the Countess Erdoedy, the sisters of the Count of Brunswick and many others. It is interesting to note the affectionate familiarity which these ladies permitted him. Taking into account the extreme sensibility of the artistic temperament and the sentimental character of the Germans, it is still surprising to meet with a letter to the Countess Erdoedy, which he begins: "Liebe, liebe, liebe, liebe, liebe Graefin" ("Dear, dear, dear, dear, dear Countess"), although the letter itself is simple enough and ends: "Ihr wahrer Freund und Verehrer." He begins another letter to this lady in a strain courtly and dignified, in marked contrast to the excessive warmth of the previous example: "Alles Gute und Schoene meiner lieben, verehrten, mir theure Freundin, von ihrem wahren und verehrenden Freund." The Countess Erdoedy, who is described as being witty, cultivated and beautiful, exercised a very strong fascination on the susceptible heart of our master, and on her side, she seems to have been powerfully drawn to him. The friendship lasted many years. Music, the bond that united them, sanctified their intimacy and kept it always on a high level. Beethoven lived at her house for a time. He used to allude to her as his father confessor. Madame Erdoedy erected in honor of Beethoven, in the park of one of her seats in Hungary, a temple, the entrance to which is decorated with a characteristic inscription expressing her homage to the great composer. Later in life she was banished and died in Munich.

The Baroness Ertmann was also a good friend to Beethoven. He called on her frequently and her ability to interpret his works acceptably must have cemented the friendship between them. Others with whom he came in contact were the Countess Babette de Keglivics (Princess Odeschalchi), and Julia Guicciardi, who became the Countess Gallenberg, and to whom he dedicated the Sonata Fantasia, which is called the language of resignation.

These people on the whole were quite democratic in their relations toward artists. There was a very elaborate cere-monial at court, but elsewhere, cultivated people met on common ground. Ries relates an incident illustrating the cameraderie existing between Beethoven and the aristocratic ladies of his circle. In this instance. Princess Lichnowsky, who was a Countess Thun, and connected with some of the best families in Europe, was the central figure. One evening at Count Browne's, Ries was asked to play a sonata with which he was not familiar. Ries preferring to play something else, begged to be excused from playing this particular one. The company was obdurate, however, and finally appealed to Beethoven, knowing that he, if any one, could carry the point. Beethoven turned to Ries and asked him to play it, saying: "I am sure you will not play it so badly that you would not want me to hear it," whereupon Ries complied,

Beethoven turning the leaves for him. He made a break in the bass part, at which Beethoven tapped him on the head with his finger, whether to discipline him or only in play does not appear. Later in the evening Beethoven played a sonata (opus 21), entirely new, with which he himself was not very familiar. Princess Lichnowsky, who had observed Beethoven's act in disciplining Ries earlier in the evening, stationed herself back of Beethoven's chair, while Ries turned the pages. When Beethoven made a mistake similar to that of Ries, the Princess playfully hit him several taps on the head with her hand, saying: "If the scholar is punished for making a slight mistake, the master should not escape, when making a graver one," at which all laughed, Beethoven taking the lead. Then he began again and fairly outdid himself, particularly in the Adagio, in which the mistake occurred.

The virtuosity of some of the Viennese of the period was marvellous. Allusion has been made to the ability of the professional musicians, but the amateur performers were in many cases equally proficient. It is related that Beethoven's friend, Marie Bigot, played the Appassionata Sonata at sight from the manuscript for the delectation of some friends. Madame Bigot was the wife of the librarian of Count Rasoumowsky and evidently took a prominent part in these entertainments. Sight-reading before a critical audience is surely a difficult enough task under the most favoring conditions; how much more so from the manuscript, with its excisions and corrections and general indistinctness! It was, however, an every-day matter especially in chamber-music. Huemmel is reported as saying: "In Vienna there are a hundred ladies who can play the piano better than I." Another musician, writing from Vienna in 1820, said: "In every house there is a good instrument; at one, a banker's, there are five."

On one occasion, some one laid before Beethoven a quartet in manuscript which had just been composed. The band essayed it, of course at sight, not one of the party having seen the manuscript before. The cellist got out in the first movement. Beethoven got up, and while he kept on playing his own part, sang the cellist's part. When this was commented on, he remarked that the bass part *had* to be this way if the composer understood his business. The composer in this instance was Foerster, his old teacher.

On another occasion, Beethoven played at sight a new and difficult composition which had been brought him. The composer told him that he (Beethoven), had played the Presto so fast that it would have been impossible to see the single notes. "That is not necessary," Beethoven replied. "If you read rapidly, many misprints may occur; you do not heed them, if you only know the language." Wagner in his life of Beethoven says: "The power of the musician is not to be appreciated otherwise than through the idea of magic." It would seem so in very fact. Consider the million combinations of which the brain has to take cognizance while doing so comparatively simple a thing as transposing. Not to play the particular notes which are indicated on the staff, but some others, one or two steps higher or lower; to play four or five at a stroke, as in piano, and to do it quickly, sixty or eighty or a hundred in a minute,—this is almost like magic, but it is nothing to what Beethoven frequently did in music. At a public concert at which he played, he asked his friend Seyfried, a distinguished composer and all-round musician, to turn the leaves for him of a new concerto written for the occasion. "But that was easier said than done," said Seyfried who told the story. "I saw nothing but blank leaves with a few utterly incomprehensible Egyptian hieroglyphics which served him as guides, for he played nearly the whole of the solo part from memory, not having had time to write it out in full; he always gave me a sign, when he was at the end of one of these unintelligible passages." Seyfried, thorough musician that he was, understood the difficulties of the position for Beethoven, and was so apprehensive of turning a page at the wrong time, that his nervousness was observed by the master, who afterward rallied him about it. Extempore playing is not to be compared with this, as the concerto was written for strings and piano, Beethoven taking the piano part.

The three quartets, opus 59, known as the Rasoumowsky Quartets, to which a passing reference has been made, take their name from having been dedicated to Count Rasoumowsky, who was the Russian ambassador. The Count had married a sister of the Princess Lichnowsky and was a cultivated man whose greatest delight was music. He lived in great state in a palace, then on the outskirts of Vienna, now used as the Geological Institute. He was closely identified with the musical life of Vienna, and shortly after these quartets appeared, formed a string quartet of distinguished musicians, which he maintained for many years, taking the part of second violin himself. It is almost needless to state that Beethoven's work took precedence in the repertoire.

The first of the three quartets, the one in F, has an Adagio movement on which Beethoven inscribed in the sketch-book, "Eine Trauerweide oder Akazienbaum aufs Grab meines Bruders." [A weeping willow or acacia tree over my brother's grave.] Beethoven had indeed lost an infant brother twenty-three years before this event, but it is not likely that he was thus tardily commemorating him. His brother Kaspar Karl was married the day before this quartet was begun and it is probably a humorous allusion to that circumstance. But if his brother's marriage was an occasion for humor at the beginning, it lapsed afterward into the sternest tragedy in its effect on the master's life, as will be seen further on in these pages.

These quartets are monuments to Beethoven's genius and are classed among the best examples of chamber-music. The Adagio of the second one was thought out by Beethoven one night while contemplating the stars. Somewhat of the infinite calm and serenity of his mood is imparted to it. The incident is related by Czerny to whom it was related by Beethoven himself. The quartets were generally disliked and condemned by musicians when first produced. Cherubini said that they made him sneeze. Others said that Beethoven was music-mad, that they could not be called music, that they were too difficult, unintelligible, and so on. That was close onto a century ago, and they are still unintelligible to some, but we now know that this is not the fault of the quartets as was so naively assumed at that time. The condemnation of them by the performers has a show of reason in it as they taxed their capacity too severely. Wagner had the same thing to contend with for the same reason.

After the withdrawal of Fidelio, noted in the last chapter, and with the advent of summer, Beethoven left Vienna on a visit to Count Brunswick, at his seat in Hungary. The Count was a man of exceptional intellectual ability, who had the greatest reverence and admiration for Beethoven's genius. Beethoven was also on excellent terms with the Count's sisters, and later became engaged to one of them, the Countess Therese. It is well known that the Countess Therese exercised a powerful fascination over him, but so did many another of the gifted Vienna ladies in the course of his life.

So vast a quantity of work was accomplished by the master during this summer, that it is likely the proximity of these friends only served to stimulate his genius. The Appassionata Sonata was worked over, the Rasoumowsky Quartets were finished, as well as the Fourth Symphony, besides lesser works, so that he could not have spent much time in social intercourse. He was in the period of his greatest productivity;

the creative instinct was strong in him and impelled him onward in his work to the exclusion of other desires. Even friendship had to give way in great measure to the passion for creating which had become a necessity of his existence.

That the life was a tranquil and contented one may be inferred by the character of the Fourth Symphony. Beethoven loved country life, and surrounded as he was by his friends, whose first thought was for him, he had everything to make him satisfied. The serenity which speaks to us through the Fourth Symphony is something for which the world should ever be grateful. Our highest happiness often comes to us through the frame of mind superinduced by external influences. This symphony is a song of joy, ecstatic in its pure exuberance of spirits; again, it is a benediction that breathes into our minds somewhat of its own spirit of calm and content. The storm and stress of life is forgotten; all is holiday humor. We are in the midst of a Shakespearian comedy, with its alternations of humor and sentiment, its joyous atmosphere, its idyllic simplicity; the forest of Arden has come to us. It was written to celebrate his engagement to the Countess Therese. In it he is inspired by the very genius of happiness. It is as if, having obtained his heart's desire, he invites us to partake with him the joy that the gods have provided.

But it is only for once, as if to emphasize the fact that happiness is not the object of existence and is not even our right primarily. He gives few instances in which the element of pain or sadness does not enter to some extent. His works abound in psychological suggestion; they illustrate every phase of life. The philosophic import of the Fourth Symphony is plain. He demonstrates the rarity of pure unalloyed happiness in actual life by the few examples in his compositions in which it reigns supreme. Joy enters incidentally into most of his works. Often it dominates them.

He recognized it as part of the scheme of life, but it is usually qualified by other conditions and is only attained through persistent effort; it is never our portion until earned. It does not come unsought like pain and suffering. The Fourth Symphony is lighter than the "Eroica" which preceded it, or the C minor which comes next. The language of joy is always more or less superficial. The tragedies of life have to be told in stronger language, since they go deeper. Happiness is negative, pain positive. The comedies of Shakespeare, in which the note is usually buoyant and felicitous, do not stir us as do the tragedies.

Beethoven's visit at Count Brunswick's continued throughout the summer of 1806. He left the Brunswicks in October, but instead of returning to Vienna as was his wont in the autumn, he turned his face toward Silesia, on a visit to Prince Lichnowsky who had an estate there. But the idyllic life left behind at Count Brunswick's was not to be repeated here. His stay was destined to be short owing to a violent quarrel between the Prince and him, which caused an estrangement lasting some years. The circumstances leading up to it can be briefly narrated. When Beethoven arrived at the castle of Prince Lichnowsky, he found other guests there, uninvited but not unexpected, consisting of French officers who had been quartered on the Prince. Napoleon had overrun Germany, and was master wherever he went. Beethoven's rage against him for making himself Emperor had not abated; his dislike extended to the officers as well, and he was not there long before hostilities began in good earnest. It all came about from a desire on the part of the officers that Beethoven play for them. He had the penetration to know that he was regarded simply as a curiosity, that he was called on because no better entertainment was available. Had there been a juggler or a ballet-dancer on hand, these latter might have been preferred. At dinner, a staff-officer had asked him quite innocently if he could play the cello, to which no answer was given; the frown on Beethoven's face, however, boded ill for the evening's festivities. It had been announced that he would play for them, and they expected it as a matter of course.

In the nature of things it could not be expected that these men would be able to appreciate Beethoven, or understand much of his art. His reverence for it was great; he felt that it would be a degradation, in a sense, to play for them under the circumstances, and refused. The Prince, with the amiable desire of pleasing his guests, urged the matter, but Beethoven continued obdurate; upon which he told him, probably by way of a joke, that he must either comply or that he would be confined in the castle as a prisoner of war for disobeying orders. This persistence so enraged him that, although it was night, he left the castle without the Prince's knowledge, and walked three miles to Trappau, the nearest post-town. He remained here overnight, and, while waiting for the post-chaise, wrote the following letter to Prince Lichnowsky:

"Prince! what you are you owe to chance and birth. What I am, I am through myself. There has been, and will yet be thousands of princes, but there is only one Beethoven."[A]

[A] Frimmel's Beethoven.

It was raining when he left the castle, and the manuscript of the Appassionata Sonata, hastily packed, became water-soaked and blurred; it bears the marks of that night's journey to the present day.

Some difficulty was experienced in procuring his passport for Vienna. It could readily have been obtained by having recourse to Prince Lichnowsky, but Beethoven would not permit this. The matter was finally arranged, and he proceeded on his journey. He nursed his wrath all the way, and on reaching his quarters in Vienna, his first act was to smash a bust of the Prince which stood on a bookcase.

Although a reconciliation was effected later, the old cordial relations were never restored. There were times when the Prince called on Beethoven and was not received, when the latter was not in the mood for seeing him. Through his wilfulness, Beethoven lost the annuity which the Prince had settled on him on his coming to Vienna. The initiative in this matter was probably taken by Beethoven himself, as may be inferred from a letter he writes to a friend two years later: "My circumstances are improving without having recourse to people who treat their friends insultingly."

The winter of 1806-7 was a period of great activity for Beethoven, although a felon on his finger must have stopped all work for a while. Some important works were published, notably the Eroica Symphony and the Appassionata Sonata. Along with acceptances came commissions, so that his finances appear to have been in a flourishing condition for the time.

Beethoven's engagement to the Countess Brunswick was entered into with the consent of her brother. Count Brunswick, who was the only one permitted to share the secret. Every precaution was taken to prevent a knowledge of it coming to the ears of Therese's mother, who would not for a moment have listened to an argument leading to a possible union of her daughter with the poor musician.

That Beethoven had marriage in mind is evident from the fact that he once got so far as to write to Bonn for a copy of his baptismal certificate as a necessary preliminary. He wrote in his note-book on the subject as follows: "Oh God! Let me attain her who is destined to be mine and who shall strengthen me in virtue." But it never got any further. The secrecy so strictly enjoined, must have been specially unpleasant to a man of Beethoven's temperament. The opposition that was sure to be developed on the part of the Countess's family may have reverted on his sense of pride to such an extent as to lead him to sacrifice his love to it. He always had his work to fall back on. In the end, his art took precedence of all other considerations; while it permitted friendship, the serenity of which might aid him in his life-work, it excluded love, which might become a rival. His concept of life was to live simply, to entertain no project which would in any way divert his mind from his work. No mere desires of self were to be considered.

The Countess Therese never married, but occupied herself with philanthropic work on reaching middle-age. She founded a home for little children in Vienna, the first of its kind in Austria; her own means not being sufficient to maintain it, she enlisted the support of powerful friends from the Empress down, in its behalf. She died in 1861, aged 83.

CHAPTER VII

VICTORY FROM DEFEAT

To those whom heaven favors, the greatest evils turn to greatest good.

—GIORDANO BRUNO

Of the summer of 1807, the most notable achievement is the Mass in C. It was written at Heiligenstadt, where he wrote the Heroic Symphony some years before. He remained until autumn hard at work on this, his first mass, as well as on some orchestral works, including, probably the Symphony in C minor, as well as the Pastoral Symphony.

It is rather singular that Beethoven, whose nature was on the whole essentially religious, although he affiliated with no church, did not take earlier to mass composition. Some of the best work of Mozart and Haydn is in this form; as organist he must have been familiar with their masses. One can readily believe that the emotional quality of certain portions of Mozart's Mass in B flat, such as the Et incarnatus and the Agnus Dei, must have strongly appealed to him. His thoughts often went toward religious music, and it was easy for him to compose in this style. He recognized the mass as one of the great art-forms, equal to the oratorio or the opera. From Bach's time on, it may indeed be said to have been regarded in this light. It is quite evident that Bach so considered it when composing his grand mass in B minor, which in difficulty of execution, as well as in its extraordinary length, is no longer practicable as a church service, its range in all directions going beyond the requirements of a congregation, or the capacity of the choir.

It is evident that Beethoven enjoyed working on the Mass, and was quite at home in this form of composition. Here was plain sailing; he knew what he wanted to do, and went at it without hesitation. There is none of that doubt and groping which is the case with Fidelio, which was continually being worked over, and in reality, never was finished. That religious works had a great hold on his mind, appears from a letter to his publisher in after years in which he states that if he had an independent income he would write nothing but grand symphonies, church music and perhaps quartets. In another letter dated March 29, 1823, toward the close of his life, he stated his intention of writing three more masses.

In the Mass in C a new theory is developed in mass composition. It differs radically from the style of church composition made popular by Haydn and Mozart, beautiful as some of that is. Their music is a concord of sweet melodies, illustrating the peace and happiness which a contemplation of the religious life affords. Acting on the principle that beauty is its own excuse for being, they give many examples where the music does not even attempt to fit the sentiment of the words. The Kyrie of Haydn's Imperial Mass would do for a Te Deum, or a Song of Triumph rather than a cry for help. The Kyrie of Mozart's Mass in B flat is an Italian street song which he heard on one of his tours in Italy and worked over for this Mass, and is not at all adapted to the words. There are ideas in the Mass in C which neither

Mozart nor Haydn would have tried to attain. Beethoven's aim here is not to please the ear by beautiful melodies, although he does that often enough, but to stir the soul. He bears a message to the listener, which it is greatly to his interest to get at. The Mass in C depicts our innermost experiences. It has a mission and is not simply an end in itself. The Symphonist here shows his individuality as may be expected, since it was composed after Coriolanus, the first four symphonies, Fidelio. In many places the orchestra becomes an independent entity, abandons the choral part, and, rising into majestic strains unattainable in choral composition, tells the story of Christianity in its own powerful way. In Beethoven this ascendency of the orchestra is first apparent; he has demonstrated for all time its greater importance as a means of musical expression than the voice.

The work throughout is cast on a higher plane than any mass which had appeared since Bach's Mass in B minor. It was written for Prince Nicholas Esterhazy, whose grandfather was Haydn's patron, and was first sung in the chapel of the Prince at Eisenstadt, on the name-day of his wife, the Princess Marie. Huemmel was Kapellmeister there, but Beethoven conducted the performance on this occasion.

The Prince evidently was of the opinion that having ordered the work, the master would consider his preferences and prejudices in the composition of it, as Haydn would have done, but as Beethoven could not have done, had he wished. The result was that Prince Esterhazy failed to see its purport or significance and was unable to comprehend it. Beethoven should not have been surprised at this, since he knew himself to be in advance of his time. At the conclusion of the service the Prince made the rather inane remark, "but my dear Beethoven, what have you been doing now?" in allusion to the mass. Beethoven, deeply offended, left abruptly, and returned to Vienna. It may be said in passing that Beethoven frequently managed to disappoint the persons for whom he wrote. This did not lead him to doubt or distrust his powers, knowing intuitively that posterity would justify him. The Mass in C is to-day one of the best known of all masses, and is frequently performed at high festivals in churches having a good equipment of chorus and orchestra.

Another great work which was completed about this time was the Symphony in C minor (The Fifth). Here we have a work wholly subjective. It reflects his soul experiences. His approaching deafness brought him face to face with the greatest trouble of his life. The malady progressed slowly but steadily, and rendered him at times hopeless. His suffering, his despair, his resignation and final triumph are embodied in it. It is a subtle analysis of some of the deep problems of life. The history of his own mental state is depicted here. If we consider his malady in its bearing on his life, we have the story of Tantalus told again. Here was a man whose thoughts translated themselves into splendid tone-pictures which the orchestra was to portray. With the mental equipment to create a new era in his art, the medium by which he could apprehend his works was being closed to him. "Is a blind painter to be imagined?" asks Wagner in this connection. If we can imagine a great painter painting his masterpieces, but never being permitted to see any, an analogy may be found in the exclusion of Beethoven from all participation in the rendering of his works, which was the case in his later years, being unable even to conduct them. He wanted to test his work, to ascertain how it would sound in the concert hall, and even at this time the high tones of the violins, which he put to such exquisite uses in later years, and which were such an inspiration to Wagner, were lost to him. By the aid of his philosophy, however, he accepted the situation, resolving to make the best of it; to keep on achieving, to turn his defeats into victories. Beethoven's symphonies mean much in their application to the common life of humanity. Knowing them even approximately, we often find texts which illumine them in the writings of men who went below the surface of things, Emerson, or Carlyle, or Schopenhauer. Thus Carlyle, writing on Dante says: "He has opened the deep unfathomable oasis of woe that lay in the soul of man; he has opened the living fountains of hope, also of penitence." Does not the mind instantly revert to the C minor Symphony?

Next in the order of Beethoven's great works comes the Pastoral Symphony, named at first "Recollections of country life." Easily comprehended, as any picture of country life should be, he yet deemed it necessary to give a short explanation at each movement, illustrating the meaning which he wished to convey, although he qualifies this with the words, "mehr Ausdruck der Empfindung als Malerei." [An expression of sensibility rather than painting.] In everything relating to his art Beethoven was tentative. In the sketch-book of this Symphony there is an inscription in his handwriting, "Man ueberlaesst den Zuhoerer sich selbst die Situationen auszufinden." [The hearer should be left to find out the situations for himself,] showing that, on considering the matter carefully he changed his mind, and concluded after all, that the explanations were permissible. In but few instances has Beethoven vouchsafed any explanation of his musical intent, and then it seems to have been done reluctantly. It was hardly necessary in the case of the Pastoral Symphony as it is comparatively easy of comprehension. The title gives the clew; the occasional bird notes of quail, cuckoo and lark, the scene at the brook, could hardly be mistaken; while the dance-music in Part III, as well as the storm with its forebodings of terror, convey their meaning plainly to the average intelligence. This poem of nature is always enjoyable, refreshing the mind, and resting the jaded faculties, much as a trip to the country helps us physically.

The explanations as Beethoven appended them are as follows:

No. I. Allegro: The awakening of cheerful feelings on arriving in the country.

No. II. Andante: Scene at the Brook.

No. III. Allegro: Merry meeting of country folk.

No. IV. Allegro: Thunder-storm.

No. V. Allegretto: Song of the Shepherds, and glad and thankful feelings after the storm.

Many great composers before and after Beethoven have essayed this portrayal of a storm, Haendel, Haydn (Seasons), Glueck, Mozart, Rossini (William Tell overture), Chopin, Wagner (Flying Dutchman), are a few instances.

The Pastoral Symphony has been dramatized so to speak, that is, it has been put on the stage, the different situations of this nature-poem having been portrayed by living and moving tableaux, pantomimic action and ballet; there was scenery, and the dance of the peasants and the thunder-storm were, no doubt, realistic enough. This representation took place at a festival of the *Kuenstler Liedertafel* of Duesseldorf in 1863, also in London.

CHAPTER VIII

MEETING WITH GOETHE

Eine schoene Menschenseele finden ist Gewinn.

—HERDER

Beethoven did not have the faculty of teaching except in rare instances. It is not in the nature of things that such a man would consider teaching in any other light than drudgery, and would feel that time so spent could have been much better employed in composition. This was the case already in Bonn, when he had no income and before his creative talent had shown itself. He was only too glad to abandon it as soon as proper encouragement for composition came to him from his publishers. Here and there an attractive lady would be able to cajole him into giving a few lessons on the pianoforte—the Brunswick sisters and Madame Ertmann are instances, but they were intermittent in character, and did not continue long. Two prominent exceptions, however, were the Archduke Rudolph and Ferdinand Ries. True, Czerny was a pupil also, but the lessons did not continue long, as was the case with the Archduke and Ries.

Beethoven's acquaintance with the Archduke began in the

George Alexander Fischer

winter of 1804. Rudolph, then sixteen years of age, seems to have attached himself to Beethoven, then thirty-four, more as a friend than as a pupil. Other masters could have been found under whom he would have advanced more rapidly, and it is quite likely that the Imperial family would have preferred some other than Beethoven, whose republican principles must have made him disliked by them.

The Archduke was passionately devoted to music and the friendly relations between master and pupil were maintained almost to the end of the master's life. Rudolph had to put up with Beethoven's outbreaks of temper much the same as if he had been a civilian. He treated this young Prince, brother of the reigning Emperor, much the same as his other friends, and Rudolph had to adapt himself to his master's wishes. He ordered his chamberlain to set aside the observance of the rigid etiquette of the Court, established by his mother, Maria Louisa of Spain, when he learned that it was one of the things which made Beethoven lose his temper. Some of the master's best work was written specially for Rudolph and when the latter left Vienna in 1809, Beethoven wrote the sonata, Les Adieux L'absence, et le Retour, to commemorate the occasion. He inscribed it as follows: "Der Abschied am vierten Mai gewidmet und aus dem Herzen geschrieben." Rudolph had an intuitive perception of Beethoven's greatness and was glad to be near him, not only to learn from him, but to enjoy his friendship. He carefully preserved Beethoven's letters and in every way showed his regard for him. On the high level which music made for these men, artificial distinctions were forgotten; the Prince became the disciple. He was a fine performer, with, as may be supposed, special reference to Beethoven's works. Beethoven was, no doubt, impressed by Rudolph's rank, although there is very little evidence of it in the anecdotes which we have relating to them. He met his friends on the common ground of his art, where he found no superior.

As before stated Beethoven did not take to teaching. It was *Dientschaft* to him in the full sense of the word. He does not seem to have interested himself as much in Rudolph as in Ferdinand Ries. In the case of the latter an artist was being prepared for a career; some of Beethoven's own skill as performer was being perpetuated in Ries, while with Rudolph no amount of technical knowledge would have advanced the art much. He not only accepted no payment from Ries for the lessons given him, but frequently sent him money unsolicited when he had reason to suppose he needed it. In the old Bonn days, after the death of Beethoven's mother, when the young man was in sore straits, Ferdinand's father, who was a member of the Elector's orchestra with Beethoven, had helped the latter in word and deed. Ferdinand then was but four years of age. Beethoven was famous by the time Ferdinand had reached manhood; when he presented himself to the master with a letter from his father, he was cordially received, and was soon on the footing of an intimate friend. Beethoven when giving him lessons was patient to a degree that was not natural to him. "I attribute this," he states, "as well as the long continued friendship he maintained toward me, largely on account of the esteem and regard he felt for my father. He often made me repeat an exercise ten times. The lessons frequently lasted two hours. He was not generally so particular about lapses in execution, but if I was lacking in expression, in crescendo and diminuendo, he would make me repeat the passage until he was satisfied." Ries made good use of his opportunities, and became a distinguished performer on the piano, ranking in this respect as high as any man of his time.

An offer to Beethoven of the post of Kapellmeister by the King of Westphalia, Napoleon's brother, in 1809 brought about one of the inevitable quarrels that marked Beethoven's association with his intimates. Ries was the victim this time. Beethoven's dislike of Napoleon, and the French in general, should have been sufficient to deter him even from considering the matter. The post carried with it a good salary however, 600 ducats (about $1,400), and the duties were light. It meant a comfortable maintenance with plenty of time for composing, and from this point of view, the offer had its attractions. A certain fixed income, through which he could be independent of his publishers, was what he chiefly desired. From every other point of view, however, the project must have been distasteful to him. At middle-age, the mind of such a man, occupied almost wholly with an ideal world, shrinks from encountering new and untried scenes. Had he accepted it, he probably never would have remained, as his love for Vienna and the old and tried friends left behind would have acted as a magnet irresistibly drawing him back. He seems not to have considered it seriously. As soon as the matter became known, however, the Archduke and two other of Beethoven's friends, the dashing young Prince Kinsky (who for bravery at the battle of Aspern was decorated on the field with the Maria Theresa cross by the Archduke Charles), and Beethoven's old friend Prince Lobkowitz—got together and made up an annuity of 4,000 florins, paper money. Of this sum the Archduke contributed 1,500 florins, Prince Lobkowitz 700 and Prince Kinsky 1,800. Owing to the depreciation in paper money the amount was considerably reduced shortly after, but he continued to draw from this source about $700 per year to his death according to Sir George Grove.

Beethoven delayed giving a decided answer while the negotiations for the annuity were dragging along. When it became evident that he would not accept the position, the offer was made to Ries. Some officious person informed Beethoven that Ries was trying to get the post away from him in a questionable manner. This was not true, but Beethoven broke off all relations with him and would not see him for three weeks. The anecdote as related by Ries is as follows: "After Beethoven had declined the position, I at once sought him to ascertain if he really did not intend taking the post, and to get his counsel in the matter. But whenever I called, Beethoven was not in, and my letters to him met with no response. Three weeks elapsed when I met him accidentally on the Redoubte; I went up to him and told him the object of my visits. Beethoven looked me over and said cuttingly, 'So! and do you think you could fill a post that has been offered to me?' and left me. Determined on having an understanding with him I again sought him the following morning. His servant in an impudent manner told me that Beethoven was not in, although I heard him singing and humming in an inner room, as was his habit when composing. I attempted to enter forcibly, upon which the servant took hold of me, with the intention of putting me out. I grappled with him and threw him to the floor. Beethoven hearing the noise came out in a rage. I was equally angry and heaped reproaches on his head. The master was too astonished to answer, but stood looking at me. Finally, explanations were offered and then I first learned of Beethoven's grievance against me. I had no difficulty in proving my innocence in the matter, and Beethoven, to make amends, at once left his work and went out with me to see about the position, but it had already been given out." Ries finally went to England where he acquired fame and fortune. He kept up a correspondence with Beethoven to the end; some of the master's most interesting letters are those written in his later years to his former pupil. Ries became a very prolific composer, whose works embrace almost every class of music, among which is to be mentioned several operas, oratorios, symphonies, much chamber-music, and many pianoforte sonatas, none of which, however have survived to the present day.

The settlement of the question about his remaining in Vienna, and the security of the future brought about by the annuity, had the effect of increasing the productivity of the master. The sketch-books of this period abound in studies for orchestral, chamber and vocal studies. It was characteristic of Beethoven to show in this manner his appreciation of the compliment tendered him. The year 1809 was not propitious to creative work. War raged in Vienna and vicinity. The city was bombarded by the French in May, and was occupied by them much of the summer. Several important battles were fought nearby. Contrary to his usual custom, Beethoven remained in the city throughout the summer. His residence was in an exposed position on the bastion, where he remained the larger part of the time, occasionally visiting his brother Karl, who also remained. He was at Karl's home while the bombardment was going on, and, during the worst of it, sought refuge in the cellar, where he even padded his ears to escape the noise. The terrific reports on the inflamed tissues of his ears distressed him greatly, and must have added permanent injury to the organs already in a bad condition.

That the achievement of the solitary worker during the summer was more important and far-reaching in its effects than that of the belligerents, will hardly be gainsaid. The latter wasted a lot of ammunition, destroyed human beings and property, and made a good deal of noise for the time being, after which things settled down to about the same condition as before; while Beethoven added solid wealth to the world in its most lasting form.

There is a falling off in his compositions the following year, which is generally attributed to the breaking of his engagement with the Countess Therese. That he should have suffered to such an extent on this account, is at least open to question. His art was of more importance to him than any other fact in life. It was only by a complete surrender of everything else that he achieved what he did in it. He had many bitter disappointments at different periods of his life, which, however, did not take him away from his work. At all events, he gave no sign, contrary to his usual habit. He was reticent on the subject of his compositions, but was not averse to talking of his troubles. A man so entirely given over to one idea, as was Beethoven, could hardly take such a step as marriage at the age of forty, thereby changing his whole course of life. The passion for creating had grown to such an extent, that he became impatient of everything which interfered with it. It is possible that the Countess Therese, noting this, felt that there would be little chance for happiness in such a union, and wisely broke it off. He could not have been considered eligible in any event by a family like the Brunswicks, noted for extravagant living and a desire to occupy a prominent place in society. Beethoven's income was never large. It was at times insufficient for his simple wants, owing to his ignorance of the value of money. That he managed to fall in love with a frequency only equalled by his impetuosity, must be admitted. But when the question came fairly before him, marriage or music, he had but one course. His art was a jealous mistress which would brook no rival. If he took the breaking of his engagement so much to heart that it interfered with his work, how was it possible, we may ask, for him to have made violent love to Bettina Brentano during this summer of 1810? Within two years afterward he was as badly smitten with Amalie Seebald the singer. We can only reiterate the former statement, music was his one passion, in this he was supreme. His art had so strong a hold on him that nothing else could come between. These love affairs were episodes in his social life. They were as episodical with the ladies concerned, who later, generally married in their own station, and, let us hope were happy ever afterward.

The artistic temperament will account for these rhapsodies. Ill health in this period probably had as much to do with his lessened productivity as anything else. Schindler states that he had been on bad terms with his stomach for many years of his Vienna life. Confirmation of this is to be found in Beethoven's letters in which complaints about stomach and intestinal troubles are frequently met with in these years. These gastro-intestinal disturbances which so afflicted him had their origin in the chronic liver trouble to which he finally succumbed.

In the spring of 1812 he resolved by the advice of his physician to try the baths of Bohemia, and we find him at Toeplitz, one of many notabilities, who were spending the summer at this place. Here he made the acquaintance of Goethe whom he held in great esteem. It was here also that he met Amalie Seebald of whom mention has already been made. She was a fine singer, and a beautiful, amiable woman of considerable talent. Beethoven wrote the following in her album:

Ludwig van Beethoven
Den Sie wenn Sie wollten
Doch nicht vergessen sollten.

Ludwig van Beethoven
Whom if you would
Forget, you never should.

It may be said in passing, that she was not the last to whom Beethoven yielded his susceptible heart. It would make a long list were it arranged chronologically, from the early Bonn days to his forty-fifth year.

[Transcriber's note: The letter reads thus (words that I'm not sure of are marked with asterisks) "Es geht schon liebe A. besser wenn Sie es anstaendig heissen, allein zu mir zu kommen, so koennen Sie mir eine grosse Freude machen, ist

[a]ber dass Sie dieses unanstaendig finden, so wissen Sie, wie ich die Frejheit aber Menschen ehre, und *wie Sie dies *heuer hierin und in andren Faellen handeln moegen nach ihren Grund fuer zueinander wie Muehe, mich finden Sie *nur gut und als "Ihren Freund Beethoven"]

An incident of his visit at Toeplitz, showing Beethoven's humility and kindliness will bear narrating, as it was characteristic of the man. It relates to a stern parent, a lovely daughter, an ardent wooer. The first two characters of the *dramatis personae*, were the innkeeper, at whose house Beethoven dined, and his daughter. The part of lover was taken by Ludwig Loewe, an actor, while Beethoven's part in the little drama is not much more important than that of scene-shifter. Loewe was a man in good standing, and came from a family of some prominence, but the father objected to him and forbade the daughter speaking to him. It appears that Beethoven was in the habit of coming late for dinner, so the plan was hit upon that Loewe was to take dinner late also, at which hour, the other guests having eaten and gone, and business being over for the time, the father was not apt to be around to interfere. "All the world loves a lover." Beethoven was an interested spectator of the little comedy, no doubt casting occasional friendly glances in the direction of the young couple. The father finally appeared on the scene, ordered the actor to leave the house, and forbade him coming there any more. At this crisis the lovers were in despair, that is for a while. Love laughs at locksmiths, as we know, and it had not got so far as that yet. Loewe, with the resources of a true lover, managed to meet Beethoven accidentally away from the inn, and looked at him so intently that he was rewarded by an answering nod of recognition from the master. The ice being broken, the actor disclosed his troubles. Meeting with sympathy, he was emboldened to ask him to deliver a letter to Fraeulein Therese. To this Beethoven agreed, and, taking the letter, started to go, thus closing the interview. But Loewe was not so easily gotten rid of. With an embarrassed manner, he managed to convey to Beethoven the fact that there would be an answer. "So! And you wish me to deliver it? Well, meet me here to-morrow;" and so Beethoven became the go-between for the lovers during the remainder of his stay in Toeplitz.

Allusion has already been made to the acquaintance which he formed with Goethe this summer. That Beethoven had the highest esteem for the poet, there is no doubt. In speaking of him in after years, he said, "Who can thank sufficiently a great poet? He is the most precious jewel of the nation" (kostbarste Kleinod einer Nation), which is much like Carlyle's remark on the great poet. "The appearance of such a man (Goethe) at any given era, is in my opinion the greatest thing that can happen in it. A man who has the soul to think and be the moral guide of his own nation and of the whole world." Goethe and Beethoven were on friendly terms and saw a good deal of one another during this summer. The acquaintance must have made a powerful impression on Beethoven. Goethe, the senior by many years, whose transcendent intellect had won him a world-wide reputation, was no doubt the cynosure of all eyes. Toeplitz was full of notabilities. Thayer gives a long list of prominent persons, from royalty down, who sojourned there this summer. It must have been a very agreeable experience to the younger genius, whose fame had not yet penetrated much beyond Germany, this friendship. Had he possessed a tithe of the worldly wisdom of the elder man, and had regulated his conduct in accordance with the prejudices of the other, the friendship might have continued. Much as he desired this, it does not seem to have occurred to him to even try to make a good impression. Utterly lacking in self-control, he remained the same headstrong impulsive creature, while in Goethe's company, that he had always been. Whether or not the story is true of his meeting the Imperial family while with Goethe and disdaining even to answer their salutations, walking on and compelling the party to divide so as to give him the middle of the walk, while Goethe stood aside bowing low with uncovered head,—it is nevertheless more than probable that Beethoven showed his scorn for conventionality in numerous ways, thereby calling down on himself Goethe's disapproval. Born courtier that he was, it must have been mortifying in the extreme to him to be with Beethoven and witness his rudeness and contempt for appearances.

So far as known, Goethe never had anything more to do with him after this summer. On leaving Toeplitz he writes to Zelter, Director of the Berlin Singakademie, mentioning Beethoven casually or as an afterthought, and alludes to him as an "entirely untamed (*ungebaendigt*) person." From this time on, he seems to have excluded him from his thoughts. Beethoven's music was frequently performed at Goethe's house at Weimar. We read in "Eckermann's Conversations" that on such occasions the company would relate incidents from Beethoven's life, but Goethe never mentioned him.

Poet and musician were utterly dissimilar; it is not likely that either influenced the other to any appreciable degree. "It is a great folly," said Goethe in 1824 (Conversations with Eckermann) "to hope that other men will harmonize with us. I have never hoped this. I have always regarded each man as an independent individual, whom I endeavored to study, and to understand with all his peculiarities, but from whom I desired no further sympathy. In this way have I been enabled to converse with every man, and thus alone is produced the knowledge of various characters, and the dexterity necessary for the conduct of life." It was probably in this coldly analytical frame of mind, that the great councillor viewed the composer. But it was a momentous event to the latter to know Goethe. He had before this set to music a number of his ballads and had only recently composed the music to his

Egmont. Many years afterward, in 1822, in an interview with Rochlitz who made a pilgrimage from Leipzig to make his acquaintance, he reverts to this time. "Since the Carlsbad summer when I met Goethe, I read him every day, that is when I do read. He has killed Klopstock for me, but Goethe he lives and he wants us all to live. This is why it is so easy to make music to his words."

CHAPTER IX

OPTIMISTIC TREND

Thus, with what has hitherto been effected, the clue to the labyrinth of what is yet to be done is given us.

—HERDER: *Apotheosis of Humanity*

Beethoven visited quite a number of places during the summer of 1812 in quest of health. While at Carlsbad he gave a concert in aid of the people of Baden, who had lost heavily through a disastrous fire there, on which occasion he extemporized. It seems to have been a success financially, but not artistically. In a letter to the Archduke he cites it as being "a poor concert for the poor." "Es war eigentlich ein armes Koncert fuer die Armen." This was owing to lack of time for rehearsals, and to the fact that only one other person, Herr Polledro, a violinist of Turin, took part in it. The concert was given within twelve hours from its inception, because many noteworthy guests were on the point of leaving town, and their presence was desired to insure a good attendance. The necessity must have been great to induce him to undertake it at all. His dislike for improvising for others was deep-seated, and was increased by his deafness.

　　　　George Alexander Fischer

In the fall we find him visiting his brother Johann at Linz, where he made quite a long stay. It was not alone Johann whom he was visiting; he had good friends there, among them Kapellmeister Gloeggl, whom he saw nearly every day. At the latter's request the master composed three equali for trombones for All Souls' Day, then near at hand. These equali, as it turned out, were eventually used for Beethoven's funeral. The Kapellmeister's son, then a lad of fourteen, relates an incident of this time with Beethoven as the central figure. A resident of Linz, a certain Herr Graf von Doenhoff, who was a great admirer of Beethoven, gave an entertainment in his honor. After some of his music had been rendered by others, Beethoven was asked to extemporize, which he declined absolutely to do. Shortly after he disappeared. Supper being ready a search for him was instituted, but he was not to be found, so the company, after some delay, repaired to the adjoining room. They had hardly seated themselves at the table, when they heard some one at the piano. Gradually, one by one, they found themselves in the other room, where Beethoven was extemporizing. This he kept up for nearly an hour, when, suddenly coming to a realization of the circumstances, and looking around, he saw the entire company listening in rapt attention. He at once got up from the instrument and hastily left the room, either through anger or embarrassment. Such was his haste that he ran against a table containing fine porcelain bric-a-brac, which, of course, was shattered. The Count, with easy good nature, made some reassuring remark, upon which they all made another essay at the supper.

His object in going to Linz was not altogether for the purpose of making visits. A disagreeable duty had to be performed; Johann's relations with a young woman, whom he had taken as housekeeper, had become a scandal; the good repute of the family was at stake, and Beethoven went there with the express design of putting an end to the matter.

Johann was not at all amenable to argument, and contested the elder brother's right to interfere. The dispute became so bitter that a personal combat between the brothers occurred. It finally required the combined ecclesiastical and secular authority of Linz (bishop, magistrate and police), to effect the expulsion of the lady from town. At this turn of affairs, Johann, bound to have his own way, married her.

This year saw the completion of the Seventh and Eighth Symphonies besides other important compositions; not so bad an achievement for a sick man, this record of two years' work. Sick or well, at home or abroad, his work went on; it was a part of his life, as necessary, apparently, as eating or sleeping. In size the Seventh Symphony exceeds any of the preceding ones. "Eine meiner vorzueglichsten" (one of my best), is Beethoven's statement in regard to it. Here the composer's meaning is not so readily elucidated as in the Pastoral, for instance. It means all things to all people. He usually had a clearly defined purpose or idea before him when composing, particularly in the case of his large orchestral works. Of the creations of such a man, it was to be expected that they would increase in grandeur with each succeeding one. Every great thing achieved is only an earnest of still greater in reserve. The fertility of his mind was exhaustless. As he penetrated deeper into this new world of the imagination, wider vistas were constantly being opened before his mental vision. "What I have in my heart must come out when I write," he stated to Czerny. "I never thought of writing for fame and honor." Grandeur and simplicity are prominent traits in Beethoven's character and these are exemplified in the Seventh Symphony. Wagner calls it the Apotheosis of the dance. "Der in Toenen idealisch verkoerperten Leibesbewegung," [an ideal embodiment in tones of the movements of the human form]. This dance element is the characteristic trait of the symphony; the dance element on a colossal scale. Listen to Wagner's summary:

"But one Hungarian peasant dance in the final movement of his Symphony in A (the Seventh) he played for the whole of nature; so played that who could see her dancing to it in orbital gyrations must deem he saw a planet brought to birth before his very eyes." In these later symphonies we see the beginnings of the mysticism which so profoundly influenced Beethoven in his last years, reaching its consummation in the Mass in D, the last Quartets, and the Ninth Symphony. From this period on, the picture to be drawn of him is of a man retiring more and more into himself as his growing experience with the world shows him his unfitness for it. Only in his work did he have any real reason for living. His every-day life became, for the most part, a phantasmagoria, wherein persons and events continually changed from grotesque to sublime, where nothing was stable or to be depended upon. The only reality was in his art. The consciousness that he was composing works that would go down the ages and delight many generations to come, was probably satisfaction enough to him to compensate him for anything he was called on to endure. With the progress of his deafness his inability to cope with even the ordinary affairs of life increased, and this also had the effect of withdrawing him from the world. The spiritual insight gained by years of introspection, of communion with the higher part of his nature enabled him to discover truths hidden to the consciousness of the ordinary man. "That power of shaping the incomprehensible now grows with him; the joy in exercising this power becomes humor. All the pain of existence is wrecked upon the immense pleasure derived from the play with it; the creator of worlds, Brahma, laughs to himself as he perceives the illusion with reference to himself; regained innocence plays jestingly with the thorns of expiated guilt; the emancipated conscience banters itself with the torments it has undergone. And all his seeing and his fashioning is steeped in that marvellous gayety (*Heiterkeit*) which music first acquired through him." (Wagner.)

A peculiarity of Beethoven's work often commented on, is the extreme simplicity of his themes as they first appear in his sketch-books. These are usually elaborated, thus changing their character, taking on new meaning with the growth and development of the idea in the composer's mind; when through with it, however, the thought appears fresh and spontaneous, such was his consummate art, as if it had never undergone any elaboration. But sometimes the theme maintains its original simplicity, and the masterwork appears in the orchestration which surrounds it; at times even this maintains an archaic simplicity. Thus in the coda of the vivace of the Seventh Symphony, a simple melody is reiterated eleven times in succession, with no other orchestration than the pedal-point on E by the rest of the instruments.

The symphonies in general are the language of a buoyant, gay, blithesome mood, as befits their design for concert use. In them, for the most part, he addresses people in their holiday humor. His experience with Fidelio may have impressed the fact upon his mind that sorrow and pain should be sparingly portrayed on festive occasions. Not so with the piano sonatas, which can be heard and studied in the privacy of one's home. Even the quartets may be placed in the category since they do not require an elaborate equipment and preparation for their production.

Take him all in all optimism prevails with him, or rather, in true philosophic spirit, he demonstrates that the sorrow, the inevitable trouble and misery of life, is more than offset by the good things the gods have provided. Life, after all, is a precious gift, which should be duly appreciated. A period of enjoyment, gayety, strengthens and fortifies the mind, and enables it better to bear the burdens when they come. The great creative genius, must perforce, in the very nature of things, be optimistic in his chosen work. He is more alive, more possessed with the belief that life with its opportunities is worth while, than is the case with the ordinary man going about his petty concerns. In common life, the busiest man is the happiest man, that is the most satisfied; and this contentment springs from the consciousness of doing something worth doing, the advantage of which will remain. With the man of genius, the feeling rises to elation, to rapture, when he considers the transcendent, imperishable nature of his work. "Dass Hervorbringen selbst ein Vergnuegen und sein eigner Lohn ist."

The Eighth Symphony which was brought out at the same time as the Seventh is the shortest by a few bars, of the nine. It was completed in about four months from the date of its inception. Here as in the Seventh, the dance element is in the ascendant, commanding, swaying everything, thus coming back to first principles, almost to the origin of the art, as an art. The dance is the primordial, autochthonic form of music; its foundation so to speak. The song had its origin in the dance as indicated by its name "ballad." It is a comparatively simple matter to trace its upward course in instrumental music, as such. It is conceivable that people from remote times on, had the faculty of originating tunes, and of humming and singing them, and dancing to them long before such things as scales and notation were conceived of. Song and dance must have come into being at the same time, and the earliest dancing was done with a singing accompaniment. As people advanced in the art and became able to manufacture instruments with which to produce music to dance by, it is readily apparent that those persons who did not dance, derived pleasure from listening to it. The next step was to play these dance tunes without dancing. This naturally led to a collection of dance tunes. By playing three or four in succession it was soon found that a more agreeable effect was produced by selecting those differing in rhythm. Here we have the suite, the earliest orchestral form. After a while it was found that a change of key heightened the effect, and, when composing purely orchestral music not intended for actual use in dancing, the more original of the composers at times allowed the strict dance form to fall into abeyance in one or two movements to enable them to try their hand in another style, and also for contrast. A broadening and augmenting of the different forms and we have the sonata. The symphony is an enlargement of the sonata. All our intellectual progress is an unfolding, like a flower from the bud. We have first an impression, then an opinion, then demonstration.

Many years were to elapse before the next and last symphony was to appear; years in which the ripening process was to go on, and which were to culminate in the Mass in D, the Choral Symphony and the last quartets,—works that are in a class by themselves in the same sense that the works from the Third Symphony on, up to, and including the Eighth, are in a class apart from the others. His compositions prior to the Third Symphony are in the style of Mozart and Haydn. They are the naive utterances of the young musician who does not yet realize that he has a mission to perform; whose ambition was to be ranked with his great predecessors. Of the works of the second period, it can be said that their most prominent characteristic is gayety (*Heiterkeit*). They are not all in this mood, and but rarely is the mood maintained throughout a single work, but it exists to the extent that it dominates it, just as the key-note to his later works is to be found in his mysticism. The works of the second period are coincident with his best years physically and when his mental powers had reached their highest maturity. When he found out what manner of man he was and realized the place he was destined to occupy among the great ones of earth; when he had accepted his destiny and had made his peace with himself it is easy to understand how a certain gayety and serenity should have spread itself over

George Alexander Fischer

his life and have communicated itself to his works; and though this serenity was alternated by periods of despair, he allowed no more of this to appear in his work than his esthetic sense approved of. Like all highly organized people he sounded the gamut of joy and sorrow. His journal entries tell the story. One day, exulting in life and its possibilities he writes, "Oh, it would be glorious to live life over a thousand times." At another time he calls upon his God in abject despair to help him through the passing hour. At one time life is so difficult a problem that he sees not how it can be continued at all. Then he loses himself in his creations and soars into regions where his troubles cannot follow. This joyousness is the portion of many extraordinary people. Haydn and Mozart had it. "He has among other qualities that of great joyousness," says Carlyle, in speaking of Richter. "Goethe has it to some extent and Schiller too. It is a deep laughter, a wild laughter, and connected with it, there is the deepest seriousness."

CHAPTER X

AT THE ZENITH OF HIS FAME

Fate bestoweth no gift which it taketh not back. Ask not aught of sordid humanity; the trifle it bestoweth is a nothing.

—HAFIZ

Napoleon's star, hitherto so uniformly in the ascendant, was now on the wane. His victories at the battles of Luetzen and Bautzen in May of 1813, could not atone for the disaster of Moscow in the previous year. The crushing defeat encountered by the French at the battle of Vittoria by the English under Wellington, and the battle of Leipzig in October of the same year showed the world that here was only a man after all; a man subject to the usual limitations and mutations of mankind. The demigod was dethroned, the pedestal knocked from under, and all Europe rejoiced. The nightmare of fear which had so long pervaded all classes, was after all only a bad dream; the incubus could be shaken off, and mankind again resume its normal mode of living. Waterloo was already foreshadowed in the events of this year, and the people were wild with joy.

George Alexander Fischer

The alliance which followed Napoleon's marriage to the Austrian Archduchess did not have the good political results which Metternich expected from it. The war indemnity of fifteen millions of dollars, the cession of provinces whereby three and one half millions of people were lost to Austria, the reduction of the army to 150,000 men, exactions made by Napoleon at the time of the marriage, did not tend to make him popular. The alliance existed in name, not in sentiment. He was still regarded as the conqueror, not the ally. Austria had been lukewarm all along, and when she changed front in 1813, and joined the coalition against him, acting in concert with England, Russia and Prussia, the measure had the moral support of the nation. This was three years after his marriage to the Archduchess.

The news of the battle of Vittoria reached Vienna on July 13. Beethoven was importuned by a clever friend, M. Maelzel, a musician, to write a symphony in commemoration of it, and to call it "Wellington's Victory." Maelzel was a man of remarkable mechanical ingenuity. He had before this won his way into Beethoven's good graces by making him an ear-trumpet, which he used for several years. He was the inventor of the metronome and a man of considerable intelligence. He had invented a Panharmonicon, an auto-maton instrument containing most of the instruments found in full orchestra, on the principle of the modern orchestrion. Allied to his talents as musician and inventor were those of good business ability and a knowledge of human nature. The Battle Symphony appears to have been written originally for the Panharmonicon. "I witnessed," says Moscheles, "the origin and progress of this work, and remember that not only did Maelzel induce Beethoven to write it, but even laid before him the whole design of it; writing the drum marches and trumpet flourishes of the French and English armies himself, giving Beethoven hints how he should herald the English army by the tune of 'Rule Brittania;' how he should introduce 'Malbrook' in a dismal strain; depict the horrors of the battle, and arrange 'God Save the King,' with effects representing the huzzas of the multitude. Even the idea of converting the melody of 'God Save the King' into a subject of a fugue in quick movement emanates from Maelzel." It is hardly conceivable that Beethoven, if left to himself, would have produced anything of this sort. But it exactly suited the popular feeling, and was such a success that Beethoven was induced to arrange it for full orchestra. This work is never classed among his symphonies, although it served to make him very popular with the Vienna public.

The presence in their midst of the composer of the Eroica Symphony in these stirring times, was a significant fact, which was bound to be duly exploited by the Viennese. The Battle Symphony confirmed and emphasized Beethoven's stand as a patriot. He was consequently greatly looked up to by the young men of the time, in particular by the student element, already of considerable importance in Vienna, who made an idol of him. He was now everywhere in demand, his music of necessity being a part of the programme of every concert or important event in the City.

It is a national characteristic with the Germans to celebrate every issue with music. A great occasion called for a great demonstration. When therefore, it was proposed to give a concert in aid of the Austrian and Bavarian soldiers disabled at the battle of Hanau, where the French were intercepted after their retreat from Leipzig on October 30, the matter was intrusted to Beethoven as being the man best fitted for the work. It was stipulated that Beethoven's music was to occupy the programme exclusively, which gave him a good opportunity to produce the Seventh Symphony, still in manuscript.

An aggregation of eminent musicians volunteered their

services for the occasion, sinking their differences in patriotic elation. Moscheles, already then a great pianist, played the cymbals. Meyerbeer presided at the big drum. Spohr took a prominent part, together with Salieri, Romberg and Huemmel. The fact that Beethoven conducted it indicates that his deafness could not have been so bad at this time. The concert took place on December 8, and, as may be supposed, was a brilliant success. It was repeated four days later. At each performance, the principal event, was, not the Seventh Symphony, but rather the Battle-piece, which, performed by full orchestra for the first time, won loud and frequent applause.

After the second performance Beethoven gave a letter to the public in which he says, "The concert was a rare assemblage of eminent performers, each glad to contribute by his presence and talents something towards the benefit of the country, even to the extent of taking subordinate places in the orchestra where required. On me devolved the conduct of the whole, because the music was composed by me. Had it been written by any one else, I would as cheerfully have taken my place at the big drum, for we were all actuated by the feeling of patriotism and the desire to benefit those who had sacrificed so much for us."

The concert had to be repeated in January and in February following, as patriotism was still the ruling idea with the populace. At the February concert the Eighth Symphony was on the programme, but in each case the *piece de resistance* was the Battle Symphony. It was produced again in March, when Beethoven conducted it, together with the Egmont Overture, at the annual concert for the Theatre-Armenfonds. The symphony soon found its way to England and enjoyed great popularity there from its connection with Wellington. It frequently appeared on the programmes under the name of Wellington's Victory.

The general esteem in which Beethoven was held by the Viennese led to a demand for another hearing of Fidelio, which had been out of sight and mind for eight years. The libretto was again worked over (this time by Treitschke), and submitted to Beethoven. The revised form seems to have pleased him at once, although very important changes were made which imposed on him a herculean task. New music had to be written for certain portions, and the whole rearranged and adapted to the new conditions. Everything was going Beethoven's way in these years, which may explain his good-natured acquiescence in these demands. "Your revision suits me so well," he wrote Treitschke, "that I have decided once more to rebuild the desolate ruins of an ancient fortress." This time the opera was a pronounced success, although alterations and emendations were in order more or less during the entire season. On July 18, it was performed for Beethoven's benefit. Moscheles made a piano arrangement of the score, and must have considered it a great task, as he wrote at the end.

FINIS.
WITH GOD'S HELP.

When Beethoven saw this he wrote underneath, "Oh man, help thyself!" The piano arrangement was dedicated to the Archduke and published in August.

The year 1814 was a memorable one for Beethoven. Important events crowded fast on his horizon, chief of which were those proceeding from the meeting of the Congress of Sovereigns in Vienna in the autumn of this year. Napoleon was in the toils; he had been forced to abdicate and was now a prisoner on the island of Elba. When the treaty of peace was signed at Paris on May 30, 1814, between France and the allies, it was agreed that all the powers which had been engaged in the war on either side, should send plenipotentiaries to Vienna in general Congress to arrange for the conclusion of the provisions of the treaty of peace.

The Congress met in November of the same year, and was characterized by a degree of magnificence which renders it unique of its kind. The Emperor and Empress of Russia, the kings of Prussia, Bavaria, Denmark and Wuertemburg were present in person. England and France were represented by their highest nobles. Spain, Sweden and Portugal sent representatives. The advent of a hundred great personages in Vienna naturally brought other distinguished visitors there and the gayeties that supervened, now that the wars were a thing of the past, occupied the time and attention of the visitors to such an extent that for three months nothing of a business nature was attempted by the Congress. These were halcyon days for Vienna. Peace was restored after twenty years of such warfare as only a Napoleon could inflict, the nervous tension became a thing of the past, and sovereign and noble could again take up the chief occupation of life, enjoyment.

The city fathers, on learning that the Congress was to be convened in Vienna, commissioned Beethoven to write a cantata of welcome to honor the visitors. The poem "Der glorreiche Augenblick" (The Glorious Moment), was chosen, which Beethoven set to music. As may be supposed the new cantata served to increase his fame, although as a work of art it is about on a par with the Battle Symphony.

Beethoven occupied a prominent part in the many notable gatherings which were a feature of this winter. Associated in people's minds as a harbinger of the new era, his popularity increased in line with the ever brightening political horizon. The Archduke enjoyed having him at his receptions, introducing him to the sovereigns, and made much of him generally. It was at the Archduke's apartments that Beethoven was introduced to the Empress of Russia, who showed him much attention, both here and when meeting him elsewhere. He met her frequently at Count Rasoumowsky's, who as Russian Ambassador entertained lavishly in honor of his distinguished guests. He afterward related humorously how the crowned heads paid court to him, referring to the urbanity and courtesy which the Empress in particular, used toward him. Beethoven is on record as saying that he liked being with the aristocracy. He seems to have had no difficulty in impressing on the Empress the right concept of his importance as man and artist. In acknowledgment of the courtesies which he received from her, the master composed for her a Grand Polonaise (in C, opus 89) which, in company with the pianoforte arrangement of the Seventh Symphony he dedicated to her.

Shortly after the assembling of the Congress Beethoven gave a concert for his own benefit, at which the new Cantata as well as the Battle Symphony and the Seventh Symphony were performed. The Riding Hall, an immense structure, capable of seating six thousand persons was placed at his disposal, for which, however, a large price, one-half the receipts, was exacted, so Frimmel states. With sublime confidence Beethoven sent out invitations in his own name to the visiting sovereigns and other notabilities, all of whom responded, with the result that the hall was crowded and the concert proved to be a great success.

As a result of the winter's activities, Beethoven's finances were greatly improved. He displayed a degree of business ability during this year, which was not to have been expected from a man of his temperament. His profits from one source or another were such that he invested money to the extent of ten thousand florins, in shares of the Bank of Austria. It was his first and only investment, undertaken as a provision for the future.

George Alexander Fischer

That Beethoven kept his head in the face of all this adulation is evident from a letter written at this time to a friend at Prague in which he says, "I write nothing about our monarchs and monarchies. The intellectual realm is the most precious in my eyes, and far above all temporal and spiritual kingdoms."

It was indeed a brilliant winter, but all this joy was suddenly changed to something akin to terror by the news of Napoleon's escape from Elba in March of 1815, and that he was assembling his forces for another campaign. The gayeties had to be discontinued, the members of the Congress confined themselves to the work for which it was convened, the result being that the treaties were signed by the eight powers on June 7, upon which the Congress disbanded. This was just eleven days before the battle of Waterloo.

In November of this year Beethoven's brother Karl died, leaving the composer as an heritage his son Karl, then nine years of age. With the clairvoyance which approaching dissolution often brings, the father saw that the uncle would be a much better guardian for the boy, than the mother, and consigned him to Beethoven's care almost with his last breath. It was characteristic of such a man as was Beethoven, to accept the charge without hesitation, from an exaggerated sense of duty; to fight for its possession even, although it revolutionized his life and brought him face to face with all sorts of difficult and untried conditions.

As might have been expected, Karl's widow, who was the daughter of a rich citizen, contested his right to the control of the boy, and began legal proceedings to obtain possession of him. This was the advance-guard of a series of troubles that began to close in on him at this period, ending only with his life. Years of litigation followed, the issue being at times in favor of one side, then of the other, the boy meanwhile being in charge of the successful party. The new responsibility, assumed with scarcely a thought as to consequences, not only interfered with the bachelor habits of a lifetime, but the mental disturbance occasioned by the lawsuits which ensued, seriously interrupted his work, so that for some years very little was accomplished in the way of new compositions. "The higher a man is," said Goethe (Conversations with Eckermann), "the more he is under the influence of daemons, and he must take heed lest his guiding will counsel him to a wrong path." Could he have foreseen how this adoption of the child would interfere with his cherished work, he might have paused to consider the matter, before binding himself irrevocably by his promise to his brother.

With never a fixed habitation, no sense of the value of money, giving it away to those in need as readily as if it had no value, often enduring privation himself in consequence; with a mode of life so simple that the entire menage was frequently transported elsewhere on slight provocation, this ascetic was now to encounter housekeeping problems, make money, save it (most difficult of all), employ servants, in short undertake in middle-age and in impaired health, duties the nature of which he could not even form an estimate.

The plan of adopting the boy might not have been such a visionary one, could Beethoven have been in entire control from the start. While the litigation went on, discipline was out of the question. There were occasional victories for the mother, who then had the boy under her absolute control until such time as Beethoven was able to get the decision of the Court reversed. Even when the boy was under the uncle's charge, the mother managed at times to gain access to him in order to poison his mind against the uncle. Her influence whenever she was able to exert it was naturally adverse. That there should be a stronger affinity between mother and son, than between uncle and nephew is not surprising. She had had entire control of him up to his tenth year. She was lax in discipline and saw to it that the boy had a better time while with her than he was likely to have when under his uncle's care. That the boy began to show a preference for being with the mother can be easily understood, and it was a bitter trial to the master.

It was not alone mother-love which actuated Madame Beethoven in her extraordinary efforts to gain possession of the boy; money considerations entered into the question to some extent, as some money had been set aside for his support by the father, which she wanted to get hold of. The simple straightforward Beethoven was no match for the wiles of this woman of the world, who generally managed in one way or another to circumvent him, even to the detriment of the child. The boy was sharp enough to take advantage of the situation, and was spoiled long before the uncle was privileged legally to adopt him.

During the proceedings the case was at one time in a high court on the assumption that the "van" in Beethoven's name indicated nobility. The widow contested this, and brought action requesting that the case be tried in a lower court. When Beethoven was examined on this issue, he pointed to his head and heart, saying, "my nobility is here and here." "van" is not a sign of nobility like the German "von," and the case was sent to the lower court.

Beethoven formed high hopes on the lad's account, thinking that he would become a great musician or scholar. He had no prevision that here he was to meet with the greatest disappointment of his life. The boy was handsome and intelligent and soon won the affection of the master, who became much occupied with the interesting task of guiding his mental and spiritual development. "The heart is only for rare occasions," said Thoreau, "the intellect affords us the most unfailing satisfaction." This rather cynical observation was abundantly confirmed in Beethoven's case by subsequent developments. He wasted precious years on account of his nephew, and the anxiety occasioned by his waywardness, was no doubt one of the factors which shortened his life.

With the advent of the nephew into his life he finally abandoned all idea of marriage. In conversation with Giannatasio del Rio, who kept the school at which the nephew was placed, he stated, "I will never be able to form a closer tie than the one which now binds me to my nephew." He took lodgings near the school and visited Giannatasio's family frequently. The daughter, in her journal, published after her death, makes frequent mention of Beethoven, giving interesting glimpses into his character. She tells of his bringing violets to her on March 17, which he found in his walks in the fields, also of his carrying with him on his walks a pocket edition of Shakespeare. The sarcastic, satirical mood, which frequently took possession of Beethoven is touched on in the journal, and is illustrated in the following incident. The father on one occasion had remarked as if in compliment to the master, "My daughter plays your music," upon which Beethoven laughed outright. It is hardly necessary to say that the young lady played no more of Beethoven's music, while he was about. On one occasion, however, she was playing his *Kennst Du das Land?* when he came in unexpectedly. He recognized it, and at once went to her and stood at the piano, marking time and making suggestions in regard to the rendering of it, thus making amends for his former rudeness.

His interest in his nephew led him to make friendly advances to the father as well as to the daughters, and he spent many pleasant hours with them. On rare occasions he assumed his old air of happy boisterous humor, when young people were

George Alexander Fischer

about. He greatly enjoyed singing Goethe's "Song of the Flea," calling out as the flea is killed: "Now he'll be smashed! Now he'll be smashed!" (*jetzt wird er gegnaxt!*) making a crash on the instrument at the word "smashed."

He came to them once after Karl had been placed in another school and wept as he told them that his nephew had left him and gone to his mother. The lad was recovered by the assistance of the police, and was then placed with this family again. He once wrote a sharp letter to the father criticising his methods in the teaching of Karl, but, on reconsidering the matter sent word to the daughter asking her not to show it to her father, as it was written in a blind rage, which he now regretted. All this shows how carefully he looked after the young man's welfare. It was the same with his music, which was intrusted to Czerny. The youth inherited some musical talent and under favoring conditions might have achieved something as a musician. When the instruction began, Beethoven was in the habit of calling at Czerny's house nearly every day with his nephew. On these occasions the master would frequently improvise on the piano, to Czerny's great enjoyment. Czerny, through his devotion to Beethoven, paid particular attention to Karl, and the boy made rapid progress. He accompanied his uncle on visits to other houses, by the latter's desire, with the object of forming his taste and stimulating his ambition for the art.

From the start Beethoven planned a fine career for his nephew. "The boy must be an artist or a savant that he may lead a noble life," he said once. On another occasion, when the youth was about eighteen years of age, he said, on introducing him to a visitor, "you can ask him a riddle in Greek if you like." "My wishes and efforts have no other aim than that the boy may receive the best possible education," he wrote when contending in the Court of Appeals for possession of the boy, "as his capacity warrants the indulgence of the best hopes for his future, and that the expectation, which his father built upon my fraternal love may be fulfilled. The shoot is still flexible; but if more time be wasted it will grow crooked for want of the training hand of the gardener, and good conduct, intellect, and character, may be lost forever. I know no more sacred duty than the superintendence of the education of a child. The duty of guardianship can only consist in this—to appreciate what is good, and to take such measures as are conformable with the object in view."

The young man cared but little for this solicitude. In his uncle's home he had to study, listen to many a lecture perhaps, and do many a thing that he did not like to do. When with his mother it was different; spending-money was to be had while there and in general an easy time. No wonder that he preferred being with her. Later, when he entered the university he absented himself as much as possible from his uncle's house. Beethoven had centred his affections on the young man, and, when he remained indifferent, irresponsive, it caused him the keenest anguish. The master's letters to him from Baden are pathetic. "In what part of me am I not injured and torn?" "My continued solitude only still further enfeebles me, and really my weakness often amounts to a swoon. Oh! do not further grieve me, for the man with the scythe (*Sensenman*) will grant me no long delay." His journal entries on this account, are the utterances of a creature at bay; of a being in the last extremity. "O! hoere stets Unaussprechlicher, hoere mich deinen ungluecklichen ungluecklichsten aller Sterblichen."

It was not alone the necessity for study and other restraints, which led the young man to absent himself as much as possible from his uncle's house when he grew older and had more liberty of action. Comfortable living was not one of the factors in the Beethoven menage. Beethoven's requirements, so far as he himself was concerned, were simple almost to asceticism. He believed in discipline in the rearing of youth, but his belief in it did not extend to the point of inducing him to attempt it with his servants. The explanation of this is not far to seek. He would have had to conform to any rules made in the interest of discipline and system in the household, which would have been out of the question for him. He was wedded to an irregular mode of living and for the most part desired nothing but to be left alone. It is not surprising that the young man preferred his own quarters, to the haphazard mode of life, which characterized the master's household.

Character is never a finished product. Always it is in process of formation, of development, advancing or retrograding according to environment. Beethoven's influence, powerless during his lifetime on the mind of Karl may have been potent after death in the upbuilding of the young man's character. On arriving at years of discretion he changed his course entirely and became an exemplary citizen. As the last survivor of the Beethoven family he inherited the means of his two uncles, and settled down in Vienna living the life of a gentleman of leisure. He gave his attention to music to which he was passionately devoted, as well as to the rearing of his family, and was by all accounts a model family man. Like his illustrious uncle, he was in the habit of improvising at the piano for hours at a time.

To follow the fortunes of the posterity of great men is an interesting subject. From the researches of Dr. Vansca of Vienna, published in *Die Musik* (Berlin, March, 1902), it transpires that Karl married on July 16, 1832, a Miss Karoline Naska. Five children were born to them, as follows: Karoline, 1833; Marie, 1835; Ludwig, 1839 (named after his famous grand-uncle); Gabrielle, 1844, and Hermine, 1852. Ludwig, the only son, his military service over, married in 1865 Marie Nitche. To them a son was born on May 8, 1870, at Munich, and baptized Karl. Father and son, that is Ludwig and Karl 2d, were last heard from in 1889 in London, when the father applied for a passport to travel in various European countries. Ludwig's mother died in Vienna in 1891, at which time it was announced that the whereabouts of Ludwig and the son Karl were unknown. Efforts were then made to get news of the young Karl, who, if living, would have been a youth of twenty, but without avail, and the family are of the opinion that he died during his childhood. As far as can be ascertained at this writing the family of Beethoven on the male side is extinct.

Of the daughters of the master's nephew, Karoline and Marie married brothers, namely: Franz and Paul Weidinger. Gabrielle married a bank cashier named Robert Heimler. The youngest, Hermine, remained single. She graduated in 1889 from the conservatory at Vienna in piano and harmonium. Of the married daughters, only one, Marie, had children; a son and daughter. The only descendants of the Beethovens known to be living in 1891, are Karoline Weidinger, a widow, Gabrielle Heimler, and the son and daughter of Marie Weidinger. All these persons were at last accounts living in Vienna.

CHAPTER XI

METHODS OF COMPOSITION

A good painter should paint two things; man, and the thoughts of man's soul.

—LEONARDO DA VINCI

Beethoven usually had a definite idea before him when composing. The work progressed rapidly under such conditions. Often, however, on further consideration, a better idea would present itself in certain places on reading the work over, and these portions would have to be rewritten. He stated in this connection that he always had a picture in his mind when composing, which he aimed to reproduce in his work. "Ich habe immer ein Gemaelde in meinen Gedanken wenn ich am componiren bin, und arbeite nach demselben" (Thayer). Sometimes this picture was shadowy and elusive, as his gropings in the sketch-books show. He would then apply himself to the task of fixing the idea, writing and rewriting, until it stood out clearly in accordance with the concept already formed in his mind.

This picture, or idea, or representation, which exists in the brain of the artist, and to which he seeks to give expression in a tangible form so as to communicate it to others, is a miracle which is constantly going on in his inner consciousness. He can at will call up impressions, which immediately become objectified on the canvas of his mind, in the form of pictures. This mental process is the same in every form of creative work whether it be painting, sculpture, or any of the arts. The architect, before putting pencil to paper, will have the splendid cathedral before him as in a vision; the sculptor, the ideal form and facial expression. The mind of the artist is a vast canvas on which pictures appear, remaining a longer or shorter period at his will, and, when no longer required, giving place to others. The idea once recorded seems never to appear again. Nature is never so prodigal as with the man of genius. Of all her children he is the favorite; these pictures are given him in superfluity, out of all proportion to his ability to use them. The harder he works in the effort to catch up with his material, the more plentiful it becomes.

Mr. Chamberlain, in his Life of Wagner, calls attention to the curious fact that Wagner produced his operas in pairs for the most part, up to his fortieth year. This was true of Beethoven with his symphonies, to a great extent. He became so fired with enthusiasm while on a great work, his thoughts became so prolific, that another work must, perforce, come into being to utilize the surplus material.

This prodigality with which the artist is supplied, explains his absorption in his work. Once fairly started on a great work, this type of man carries it through with the force of a torrent. Nothing but physical exhaustion can stop him. Wagner, after completing a great work, usually had to drop all composing or writing for some months in order to recuperate. No slave-driver with a lash ever drove his victim so mercilessly as Wagner did himself when in the stress of composition. Being married he had some one to look after him, and this had an important bearing on the preservation of his health. Beethoven, with the strenuousness that came from his Rhenish ancestry, was more intractable, impatient of interference. His domestics were often afraid to go near him when engaged in composition. Usually when in deep thought he was oblivious of the outer world. He once agreed to sit for an artist, and maintained his pose for five minutes; then he forgot all about it and went to the piano, where he began improvising. This just suited the artist, who got a good position and worked along until he was tired, finally leaving the room without the master's knowledge.

The Swedish poet, Atterbohm, and Dr. Jeitteles, distinguished literary men of the period, called at Beethoven's house one hot afternoon. Their knocking met with no response, although they knew the master was in, as they heard him singing and occasionally striking a chord on the piano. Finding the door unlocked, they entered and went in search of him, finally discovering him in an inner room. He was in extreme dishabille, busily noting down his thoughts on the plastered wall. He had probably intended changing his clothes, and, while disrobing, these thoughts came crowding in on him to the exclusion of everything else. Beethoven, facing the wall with his back to the visitors, was unaware of their proximity, and they left without being discovered by him, as they did not wish to interfere with his work. This was probably in the year 1826, as Beethoven remained in Vienna all that summer, actively engaged on the great C sharp minor quartet. It may have been a part of this work which was thus produced.

Friederich Stark relates an incident that illustrates his abstraction. He called on Beethoven early one morning, and, being a friend, was given the privilege of looking him up. He went from room to room, and finally found him in his bedroom. He was just beginning to dress, his face thickly lathered with soap that had been put on the previous evening and had dried there; he had prepared to shave, but in the process had forgotten to go on with it.

His sketch-books are interesting as showing his frame of mind and temperament, while at work. In his abstraction he occasionally scribbled beautiful thoughts on the margin of his manuscripts. Thus, in the sketch-books of the Pastoral Symphony, we find this record of his joy in nature, showing how thoroughly his mind was imbued with his subject.

"Almaechtiger, im Walde ich bin selig, gluecklig im Wald. Jeder Baum spricht durch dich!"

"O Gott! Welche Herrlichkeit in einer solchen Waldgegend."

In summer he usually resorted to one of the beautiful villages in the environs of Vienna, since absorbed by the city. Thus he repaired to Heiligenstadt to write his first mass. "Oh, the charm of the woods, who can express it!" he writes, and in many of his letters from the country, he expresses his joy at being there. "No man on earth can love the country as I do. Thickets, trees and rocks supply the echo man longs for." His best ideas came to him while walking through the fields and woods. At such times his mind became serene and he would attain that degree of abstraction from the world which enabled him to develop his musical ideas. He always carried note-books and would jot down a thought as it came to him. When he got home he would elaborate it and work it into shape. He would walk for hours in all sorts of weather. Like Thoreau, he generally preferred to be alone in his walks, the presence of a companion preventing him from working out his thoughts.

Very properly, he occupied himself but little with the music of other composers. To a man of his individuality, inspiration from the outer world was not to be had or desired. His own inner wealth was sufficient. Curiously, he set a high value on

Cherubini during the period of writing Fidelio and the Third Symphony. His own creations however, were of paramount interest to him. He was a slow worker, continually polishing and improving his work up to the moment that it reached the engraver's hands.

"The Andante" said Wagner "is the typical German style." It was not Beethoven's best style. Essentially a man of extremes, he delighted in swinging the pendulum to its furthest limit either way. He early in life acquired the irrepressible joyousness in his compositions, which was Haydn's distinguishing trait. It is the key-note to much of Beethoven's work up to the time of composing the Grand Mass. It figures to some extent in his subsequent work. It is a feature which Wagner never tires of exploiting in Beethoven's work. Whenever he mentions Beethoven's name the word *Heiterkeit* (joyousness) is sure to follow. The two are almost synonymous with him. Where Beethoven is unapproachable, however, is in his slow movements, the Adagios, solemn and portentous, in which all of world-sorrow finds expression. It is in these scenes of terror that his powers stand out with supernatural clearness.

His infinitude impresses one. It is as if he had penetrated other spheres and could speak in new tongues. He delighted in startling contrasts. The Kyrie of the Mass in D has always presented itself to my consciousness as a series of gigantic tone-pictures, in which the omnipotence of God, and the impotence of humanity is brought into juxtaposition. The Coriolanus overture is another instance among the many at hand illustrating this point. Here we see how the forceful, aggressive, bold, masterful genius, is subdued by the power of conjugal and filial love, a power in this case as irresistible as that of a glacier, which will make its way against any odds. Each side in striving for the mastery, displays its own peculiar characteristics and mode. It is the everlasting struggle between the evil principle and that which is good. He ranges titanic forces in opposition and lets us see the battle. By the magic of his art we are enabled to see these pictures as on a canvas.

It is frequently stated that Beethoven's music shows a deficiency in counterpoint. His originality, the wealth of his ideas, his versatility, will explain this. The fugue, while it is ingenious and interesting, is artificial and, indeed often arbitrary in musical composition, sometimes introduced merely to stop gaps or for brilliancy of effect. It is not surprising that Beethoven should have neglected it to some extent, although he has used it with excellent effect in some of the sonatas and in his two masses. His fertility of imagination was great and it was hard for him to tie himself down to the formal style in composition, after his powers had reached maturity. The fugue, in one form or another, seems to be almost indispensable in musical composition, but it is always characterized by learning instead of inspiration. It is something which has to be worked out like a problem in mathematics. Beethoven's thought in music is marked by something higher than the disposition to divert one's attention to his talent or skill. A definite meaning is there; he has something to reveal.

At the beginning of his career as composer, Beethoven was not above taking advice on the subject of his compositions. He frequently discussed them with Prince Lichnowsky, and adopted his suggestions when it came to alterations. As he advanced in knowledge of his art, however, he became reticent on the subject and would discuss them with no one. He acted on Goethe's idea that "the greatest art after all is to limit and isolate oneself." He did not like praise or applause. Knowing intuitively that the character is endangered thereby, he sought by every means to ward it off. His improvising was such that often on leaving the instrument he would find his hearers in tears. This would embarrass him, and he would affect anger, or would laugh at them. This does not imply that he did not care for appreciation, which is quite a different matter.

He was perfectly willing to listen to censure or adverse criticism. Trifles might anger him, but this never did, and, be it said, it never influenced him either. True artist that he was, he seldom wrote down to his public. Like Wagner, he knew what was best in art, and if the public did not, he gave the matter small concern. Not for one generation are great masterpieces born. The artist lives in the future; he is always in advance of his time.

Beethoven's character was a prism of many facets. Wagner views him always as the mystic, the seer, at odds with the world. Side by side with this characterization he constantly dwells, as just noted, on Beethoven's uncontrollable tendency to humor, gayety (*Heiterkeit*) which shows itself not only in his life, but still more in his works. This may have been a device deliberately assumed to enable him to escape mental suffering. At all events it was a prominent trait of his character, but does not seem to have added to his enjoyment of life. No circumstance, however painful, but that he is able to extract some jest or pleasantry from it. The paradox is before us of a man world-weary at the core, outwardly serene, gay. In the same ratio in which those things which serve to make life enjoyable to the average man were diminished or withdrawn, does his tendency to incessant humor increase.

The consciousness of being able to achieve great things, and the joy in accomplishing them, is what gives the artist the exultant mood, the feeling of gayety. To be sensible of such an heritage, to participate in this God-given wealth, to run riot in it, to know that the more of it that is used the more will be given, to be favored of the gods in a way that the possessor of untold wealth cannot aspire to—this is what gives the serene and joyous mood, which characterizes the man of genius for the most part. When he comes out of this ideal world into the commonplace every-day life, and realizes his unfitness for it, the other side of the picture is presented to his consciousness, and then is exhibited that strange melancholy, *Weltschmerz*, which constantly comes to the fore in the journals and letters of men like Wagner, or Beethoven, or Liszt.

The Sunday morning concerts, instituted by Czerny in the winter of 1816, call for more than passing notice. A select company of professional musicians and amateurs had banded themselves into an organization for the purpose of performing and studying the best class of chamber-music with special reference to Beethoven's compositions. Czerny was the originator and moving spirit, as stated, and the performances were held at his house. Beethoven attended them frequently. Czerny, whose admiration for the master was unbounded, was brought into more intimate relations with him through these concerts, as Beethoven was consulted in regard to the programmes and occasionally rehearsed some of his new compositions with him. Though a brilliant performer, Czerny did not like public life or society, and retired from the concert stage at a time when his powers were at their best, in order to give all his time to composition. His ability in improvising was a marvel even for those times. He was Beethoven's successor in Prince Lichnowsky's circle, frequently playing at concerts at his house. He is credited with being able to play from memory all of Beethoven's works. Like Schubert, his one pleasure was to be with a few chosen spirits, and talk on the subject of his art.

In these assemblages rank was ignored. Art was a leveller, or, rather, the devotees of the art were raised to a common plane, where social distinctions were for the time being obliterated. No special invitations were required. Any one interested in the art was made welcome, and found there a congenial atmosphere. Czerny, modest and retiring, had no thought of making social capital out of these concerts. No one not wholly devoted to the art was wanted, no matter what his social position was, and want of social position was no bar when the artistic qualifications were present. It was a band of chosen spirits, and the attrition engendered by these meetings must have been advantageous to each. They were true Concerts Spirituels, an audience of artists from which the performers were drawn.

Second only to Czerny as a pianist among this company was Beethoven's friend and pupil, the Baroness Ertmann, who frequently took part in these concerts. Madame Ertmann's virtuosity has already been commented on in these pages. She won new laurels at the Czerny concerts through her admirable interpretation of Beethoven's music.

During this winter of 1816 the master composed the fine sonata in A, opus 101, for her. It commemorates the spiritual kinship existing between these two gifted persons. "My dear, valued Dorothea Caecilia," he writes in his letter of dedication, "receive now what has long been intended for you, and may it serve as a proof of my appreciation of your artistic talents and of yourself; I regret not having heard you recently at Cz—(Czerny's). My absence was owing to illness, which at last appears to be giving way to returning health." Some years previously, when the Baroness had lost a son by death during her husband's absence on his military duties, Beethoven asked the stricken woman to call, and comforted her, not with words, but in the language which both best understood. "'We will talk in music,' said Beethoven, who remained at the piano over an hour in which he said everything and even gave me consolation." The incident is obtained from one of Mendelssohn's letters.

Among the important works produced in this period may be mentioned the Sonata, opus 90, "A struggle between the head and the heart." It is dedicated to Count M. Lichnowsky on the occasion of his marriage to a singer. There was also the chorus set to Goethe's words, "A Calm Sea and Prosperous Voyage." This was written in 1815 and seven years later dedicated to Goethe. The two sonatas, opus 102, for piano and cello, one of which is called the Free Sonata, are interesting, as in them is foreshadowed the trend of Beethoven's mind toward religious music, which controlled him almost entirely from this time on.

The idea of writing another oratorio seems now to have taken possession of his mind. A preference for this mode appears in his journals and letters and was probably the subject of conversation on his part. At all events, the newly established Society of Friends of Music of Vienna (which Beethoven, with his usual aptitude for punning, used to refer to as the society of *Musikfeinde*, enemies of music) made him a proposition to write an oratorio for them, which he accepted. No stipulations were made as to subject or treatment, and the society agreed to pay the handsome sum of three hundred gold ducats, merely for the use of the work for one year. So far as known, this work was never begun. The Archduke soon after obtained his appointment as Cardinal-Archbishop, and the work on the mass for the Installation occupied Beethoven to the exclusion of other works.

The loss by death of three of Beethoven's old friends must have been greatly felt by him in these years. Prince Lichnowsky, who died in 1814, was the first, and was followed two years later by Prince Lobkowitz. Hardest of all, however, for the master was the loss of his friend, Wenzel Krumpholz, who died in 1817. His relations with the latter were more intimate than with the noblemen, and had continued without a break almost from the time of his advent in Vienna. Czerny, in his autobiography, gives an interesting picture of the devotion of Krumpholz, who attached himself to Beethoven much the same as did Boswell to Dr. Johnson. He was somewhat older than Beethoven, and his position as first violinist at the Court Theatre enabled him to be of much practical service to Beethoven, as he was widely known among the professional musicians, as well as the rich amateurs. He sounded Beethoven's praises far and wide: he encouraged him to begin composition, making propaganda for him among the wealthy dilettante, and spent a good portion of each day in his company. Beethoven, who at a later period said of himself that he was too strong for friendship, did not take kindly to this intimacy at first, but Krumpholz's persistency was not to be gainsaid. He gave him lessons on the violin, and identified himself in many ways with Beethoven's advancement. Beethoven finally became so accustomed to him, that the presence of the other did not disturb him, and he would improvise before him as if he were alone. Krumpholz though devoid of genius himself, intuitively recognized its presence in Beethoven, and led the younger man to discuss his musical plans and ideas with him. The compositions as they took form in the young man's mind, were played to Krumpholz, who advised and encouraged him. The extravagant admiration of the latter sometimes acted on Beethoven's sense of humor to such an extent that he would make fun of him, and call him his fool, but this did not deter Krumpholz, who seemed to think he had a divinely appointed task set him, in aiding the development of this young genius, and was willing to put up with some vagaries from him.

In truth, Beethoven needed a champion, for, from the first, a certain originality, a strenuousness, showed itself in his work, which put the art on a new and different footing. That the young man was reaching out for higher things his public may have been aware of, but only a few, here and there, kindred spirits, cared for this. The average person was unable to recognize any higher function in music than that of simple enjoyment; anything aside from this was irrelevant, and could but lead to deterioration. Although at the beginning of his career as composer, he made Mozart and Haydn his models, this originality showed itself, and when it was continued in subsequent works, it awoke the strongest opposition in certain quarters. The strong partisanship which Krumpholz brought to bear on the situation, was invaluable to the young man, whose views needed confirmation and indorsement. Krumpholz seems to have had an affinity for discovering talent in others. He brought Czerny, at the age of ten years, to Beethoven, who immediately recognized his genius, and offered to give him lessons. That Beethoven deeply felt the loss of his old friend and teacher is evidenced by his writing music to the Song of the monks,

Rasch tritt der Tod den Menschen an,

from Schiller's Wilhelm Tell, in commemoration of him.

CHAPTER XII

SENSE OF HUMOR

In tristitia hilaris, in hilaritate tristis.

—MOTTO OF GIORDANO BRUNO

Beethoven did not have much in the way of enjoyment, as the word is generally understood, to compensate him for the pain of existence. The resources vouchsafed others in this respect, family affection, love, friendship, generally failed him when put to the test. Out of harmony with the general order of things in the material world, the point in which he could best come to an understanding with his fellow-creatures was by the exercise of his sense of humor. The circumstances of his life tended to make a pessimist of him. He did not understand the world and was misunderstood in return. To counteract the tendency toward pessimism, his resource was to develop his sense of humor, to create an atmosphere of gayety, by which he was enabled to meet people on a common plane. But not only in the ordinary affairs of life does it stand him in good stead, this sense of humor. It comes out finely in his creative work in the sonatas and the Scherzo movements of his symphonies. He originated, invented the Scherzo, developing it from the simple minuet of the earlier composers. The primary object of the Scherzo was recreation pure and simple. It was introduced with the object of resting the mind.

The evolution of humor in music is an interesting subject of study. It is something foreign to it, an exotic, of slow growth, gaining but little in the hands of the earlier composers from Bach on. Even with Haydn it never advanced much beyond geniality. They had essayed it chiefly in the minuet, but succeeded only in producing something stately, in which the element of fun or humor, to modern ways of thinking is hardly appreciable. It found a sudden and wonderful expansion, an efflorescence in Beethoven, with whom every phase of the art was developed to colossal proportions. He has made of the Scherzo a movement of such importance that it lends a distinctive character to his symphonies. In this form he is unapproachable. In the whole range of music there is nothing like it elsewhere. It is peculiar to Beethoven, and is another example of the many-sidedness of the great composer. "Happiness is a new idea in Europe," said St. Just, speaking of the period immediately following the French Revolution. Whether or not Beethoven ever met with this remark, its significance at least was taken to heart. The word Scherz—joke, sport, is sufficiently obvious. He goes much farther at times than simply to play pranks, however. A wide range of expression is possible in the Scherzo when manipulated by a master-mind like that of Beethoven. The satirical, sarcastic humor which escaped him in social intercourse at times, is vented on a colossal scale in the Scherzo, in which he often makes sport of humanity itself, making it the subject of his jest, his ridicule—its foibles being shown up, its follies exposed. When projected in this mood, the movement calls for intellectual co-operation, and is of equal importance with the others.

Humor has been defined as the outcome of simplicity and

philosophy in the character. It can exist independently of genius we know, but genius is never without humor. In other words, wherever there is a work of genius, it transpires that the author has a fund of humor with which he occasionally enriches his work. The profoundest philosophical treatises have it. It is a part of the stock in trade of every great novelist; Fielding, Thackeray, George Eliot, Walter Scott. It frequently comes to the surface in Schopenhauer pessimist though he be; it pervades Shakespeare. Few men regarded life with greater seriousness than Thoreau, but humor sparkles all over his works. It is only where this is in excess that it detracts from the value of the work. Not important in itself when separated from the deeper work which it accompanies, it is yet, all in all, one of the infallible tests, though a minor one, of the work of any man of genius. A sense of humor exists in the man even though he keep it out of his work, if he is good for anything.

Beethoven's humor was titanic, heroic, on a grand scale, always with what might be called a certain seriousness about it like that of a lion at play. Mozart gives many instances of humor in his compositions, but with a great difference in the character. His disposition was all gentleness and sweetness, and his humor is characterized by these attributes. It is on a small scale, and though enjoyable, has nothing commanding about it. The musician, more than any artist, reflects his character and trend of life in his work.

This sense of humor, inherent in the mental equipment of Beethoven, enabled him to enjoy a joke as well as give it, to perceive a ridiculous situation and extract due amusement from it, to appropriate it wherever he found it. But singularly enough, when the point of a joke was turned against himself, his sense of humor failed him utterly. He would often become angry in such cases and the perpetrator would come in for a round of abuse which made him chary of attempting it again.

Very bad music of which there was a sufficiency already in those times, gave him great amusement, which he manifested by roars of laughter, we are informed by Seyfried, who saw more or less of him during a period covering a quarter of a century. "All his friends," says Seyfried, "recognized that in the art of laughter, Beethoven was a virtuoso of the first rank." He often laughed aloud when nothing had occurred to excite laughter, and would in such case ascribe his own thoughts and fancies as the cause. Naive and simple as a child himself, he could only see the naivete in the worthless compositions above referred to, and could not understand the small ambition back of the pitiful effort. He often unintentionally afforded equally great amusement to others by his own naivete. Thus he once told Stein, of the noted family of pianoforte makers that some of the strings in his Broadwood were out of order or lacking, and to illustrate it, caught up a bootjack and struck the keys with it. Ries states that Beethoven several times in his awkwardness emptied the contents of the ink-stand into the piano. On this same piano the master was often begged to improvise. The instrument was a present from the manufacturers, and when made, was probably the best example of its kind extant. It later came into the possession of Liszt.

Beethoven's love of a joke was such that it appears in the title to one of his works, the opus 129. It is a rondo a capriccio for piano, with the title, Die Wuth ueber den verlorenen Groschen (fury over a lost penny), of which Schumann says "it would be difficult to find anything merrier than this whim. It is the most harmless amiable anger."

Beethoven was ready in repartee, and full of resources, with a wit that was spontaneous and equal to any emergency. One

New-year's day, as he and Schindler were sitting down to dinner, a card was brought in

JOHANN VAN BEETHOVEN
Gutsbesitzer (Landed proprietor).

Beethoven took the card and wrote on the back of it—

L. VAN BEETHOVEN
Hirnbesitzer (Brain proprietor).

and sent it back to Johann. Cold-blooded, selfish, always ready to profit by his talented brother, and never caring how he compromised him, it was not to be expected that Johann would have the master's approval, or that there could be any accord between them. In any encounter, the composer generally managed to be master of the situation, through the exercise of his wit, something which the duller Johann could neither appreciate nor imitate. It may be said in passing, that the master supplied the funds which enabled Johann to start in business. This was in 1809. He made money rapidly in army contracts, a business for which he was well qualified, and finally bought an estate and set up for a landed proprietor.

Beethoven's waggishness was frequently vented on a young friend, Zmeskall, who was court secretary. Zmeskall undertook the task of keeping the master supplied with pens, which he cut from goose-quills. Beethoven used up large quantities of them and was incessant in his demands on him. A certain drollery characterizes all his letters to him. He knew how to hit the vulnerable points in the other, and they were often made the subject of attack. Zmeskall being a member of the nobility, is often addressed by him, "Most high-born of men." He was useful to Beethoven not alone on the subject of pens, but was appealed to by him for advice and assistance on all sorts of matters. Zmeskall, though a bachelor, lived in fine state, and maintained several servants. He was thus in a position to procure the right sort of one for Beethoven. Many of the letters are either on this theme or in regard to securing him another lodging. Zmeskall is his resource in many of the small matters of every-day life, perplexing to him, but simple enough to the practical man. The master's helplessness is shown with pathos and unconscious humor in the following note:

LIEBER ZMESKALL,—

Schicken sie mir doch ihrem spiegel, der naechts ihrem fenster haengt auf ein paar stunden der meinige ist gebrochen, haben sie zugleich die Guete haben wolten mir noch heute einen solchen zu kaufen so erzeigten sie mir einen grossen Gefallen. Ihre Auslage sollen sie sogleich zuruek erhalten. Verzeien sie lieber Z meiner zudringlichkeit. Ich hoffe sie bald zu sehen.

Ihr,
BTHVN

DEAR ZMESKALL,—

Won't you kindly send me the mirror that hangs next to your window for a few hours. Mine is broken. If you will at the same time have the goodness to buy me such another you will do me a great favor. Your outlay will be immediately returned to you.

Pardon dear Z my importunity. I hope soon to see you.

Your,
BTHVN

Beethoven's lapses from grammar (untranslatable into English), indicate his impatience at the trivial wants and necessities which interrupt his creative work and take his thoughts from his compositions. Instances of bad grammar in his letters are frequent, when dealing with ordinary topics. In no sense a polished man, he could, however, when the occasion required it, assume in his grammar and diction the grace and elegance of the scholar, but it does not often come to the front. He was too rugged, too headstrong, to pay much attention to the little niceties of life.

In common with his contemporaries, Zmeskall found his principal enjoyment in music. He gave musical parties at his quarters, playing the cello himself, and gathered about him many of the most distinguished artists and amateurs of the day. Beethoven was always interested in feats of virtuosity, but he cared little for the compositions of others. He occupied himself with his own work to the exclusion of that of his contemporaries. His musical library was scant, consisting of a small collection of the works of the early Italian masters, bound in one volume, some of Mozart's sonatas—which must have seemed to him curiously stunted and commonplace in comparison with his own—and a portion of Don Giovanni. In addition, he possessed all of Clementi's sonatas, which he greatly admired and which formed the basis of the musical studies of his nephew for several years. Lastly there were a few works of Bach, consisting of the Well-tempered Clavichord, some motets, three volumes of exercises, some inventions, symphonies and a toccato.

In speaking of Weber he said that he began to learn too late, and makes the curious criticism that Weber's only apparent effort was to attain the reputation of geniality. In reading Freischutz, he said he could hardly help smiling at certain parts, but afterward qualified this by saying that he could judge it better if he could hear it. Schindler says, that when Rossini came to Vienna in 1822, and endeavored to call on Beethoven, the master succeeded in escaping his visits. His opinion of Haendel is high. He once remarked to a friend who called on him, "Haendel is the greatest composer that ever lived." Continuing the narrative this friend, J.A. Stumpf of London, says, "I cannot describe the pathos and sublimity with which he spoke of the Messiah of that immortal genius. We all felt moved when he said, 'Ich wuerde mein Haupt entbloessen und auf seinem Grabe niederknieen.' (I would kneel at his grave with uncovered head.)"

Of Mozart, he said, near the end of his life, in a letter to the Abbe Stadler, "All my life I have been esteemed one of the greatest admirers of Mozart's genius and will remain so until my latest breath." Czerny said that he was at times inexhaustible in praise of Mozart, although he cared nothing for his piano works and he makes a severe criticism on Don Giovanni. "In this opera Mozart still retained the complete Italian cut and style. Moreover, the sacred art should never be degraded to the foolery of so scandalous a subject. The Zauberfloete will ever remain his greatest work, for in this he showed himself the true German composer." Of Cherubini's Requiem he said, "as regards his conception of it, my ideas are in perfect accord with his and sometime I mean to compose a Requiem in that style." (Later in life his opinion of Cherubini was greatly modified). He seldom spoke of Haydn, and had nothing of that master's compositions in his library.

Beethoven's collections in literature were far more extensive and interesting than in music. He was essentially a student. His predilections and thoughts all tended toward the acquisition of knowledge. This was a veritable passion with him. His mind ranged through almost every department of literature. In the intervals of his work, worn by fatigue, he was in the habit of resting his mind by reading the classics, or Persian literature. Schindler, who was near him for the last ten years of his life says in relation to Beethoven's love of the Greek classics. "He could recite long passages from them. If any one asked him where this or that quotation was to be found he could find it as readily as a motive from his own works." Elsewhere he says, "Plato's Republic was transfused into his very flesh and blood." He was an insatiable reader of history. As may be supposed Shakespeare was an especial favorite with him. There is a curious little work published called Beethoven's Brevier, made up of those portions of Shakespeare and the classics for which he had a particular regard. Here, Shakespeare is first on the list. There are also many selections from the Greek, and from Schiller, Goethe, Herder and others.

Although a man of considerable culture, he was not an educated man, all his available time and strength having been required for his musical training. He was, however, the equal or superior in mental attainments of any of the great musicians, with the exception of Wagner. He had the strongest faith in his own powers. It was his belief that almost anything could be accomplished by trying. Side by side with this belief was the ineradicable conviction that intellectual culture was of more importance than anything else in the universe. He stated his views finely on this subject in a letter to a young girl, unknown to him, who had sent him a present with a letter expressing her appreciation of his music. "Do more than simply practice the art (of music), penetrate rather, into the heart and soul of it. It will be found well worth while, for art and knowledge alone have the power to elevate mankind up to Deity itself. Should you want anything of me at any time, write me with entire confidence. The true artist is never arrogant; rather he sees with regret how illimitable all art is, and how far from the goal he remains. While he may be admired, he only grieves that he cannot reach the point toward which his better genius beckons him."

We read of his ordering complete sets of Schiller and Goethe in the summer of 1809. The study of these authors carried on under most unfavorable conditions, bore good fruit subsequently, as some good work was inspired by them. The Egmont music, which appeared the following year, the Calm Sea and Prosperous Voyage, Bundeslied, the different settings of Erlkoenig, the four settings of Sehnsucht are instances, although this does not by any means complete the list of his settings from the works of the authors just named.

CHAPTER XIII

MISSA SOLEMNIS

Christianity is the doctrine of the deep guilt of the human race through its existence alone, and the longing of the heart for deliverance from it.

—SCHOPENHAUER

To Christianity and the spirit of religion in man we are indebted for some of the finest arts which adorn our civilization. It was the religious principle which brought into being the temples and statuary of ancient Greece, as well as the splendid examples of Gothic architecture, which have come down to us from the middle ages. It is this which has given us those masterpieces in painting and sculpture, which have so enriched the world; but above all it has given us music, highest of all the arts. Here its influence has been most potent. Originating outside the church, it found its best development within it. Religious fervor had inspired some imperishable works of genius at a period when nothing much had yet been done in secular music. The Masses of Palestrina, the entire life-work of Sebastian Bach, the oratorios of Haendel, are cases in point. The old masters with hardly an exception gave their best thought to sacred music.

Bach has been mentioned. Haydn's important work comes under this classification. Of the works of Haendel, only those of a religious nature have survived to the present day, although he composed many operas.

The Masses and Passion-music of the old composers were often written without hope of reward, entirely from love of the subject; they were impelled to it, either through religious ardor, or from the force of their artistic perceptions. The stateliness and solemnity of the Mass, the tragic possibilities of the Passion, appealed to them, and satisfied the tendency toward mysticism, which is so often a part of the artistic nature.

As an art, music finds its best development when of a religious character. While operatic and even orchestral music in general, is written more for the sake of giving pleasure than with any clearly defined ethical purpose, the music of the Mass and Passion, religious ceremonies, entering into man's profoundest experiences, is given for spiritual enlightenment, and, being a part of the soul's needs, demands and receives higher treatment and more serious consideration than secular music. The very frame of mind which takes possession of a person while listening to music of a religious character, is favorable to a true appreciation of it. The listener is more in earnest, and the emotions called up by the subject impress him more strongly than when listening to secular music. These considerations have their influence on the composer also. We usually find in religious music of the best class, depth and earnestness of purpose commensurate with the expectation of the listener.

These few words are preliminary to a consideration of the Mass in D, the work in which Beethoven reached his culmination as an artist. He himself so regarded it, declaring it to be his greatest and best work. It is certain that he spent more time on it, and gave it a larger share of his attention than was devoted to any other of his works.

For several years prior to this, Beethoven's muse had been silent for the most part. No important work since the completion of the Eighth Symphony had been achieved, with the exception of the sonatas mentioned in a previous chapter. This was owing to the various lawsuits in which he found himself involved. His troubles had now been adjusted, however, to such an extent as to enable him to again turn his attention to large works. The pension which had been settled on him in 1809 had been imperilled by the death of Prince Kinsky and the bankruptcy of Prince Lobkowitz. The portion of it which had been pledged to him by these gentlemen had been discontinued or greatly reduced, and Beethoven had to have recourse to the law to protect his rights. A compromise was finally effected, which resulted in the pension being paid in part. Although the litigation, in regard to his nephew was still on, it was becoming more and more apparent that the outcome of it would be in his favor. His mind at rest on these points, we find him once more in good health and spirits, with creative energy not only unimpaired but greater than ever. "In general, every evil to which we do not succumb is a benefactor," said Emerson.

The announcement of the Archduke's appointment as Archbishop of Olmuetz, had been definitely made during the summer of 1818. It was well known for years previously that he would receive this appointment, and it is quite likely that Beethoven had always intended writing a mass to comme-morate it. Considering the close relations existing between master and pupil for so many years, and Beethoven's obligations to Rudolph in money matters, he could hardly have let so momentous an event go by, without writing a mass for it. A mass was probably always intended, but not such a one as eventually grew out of his original idea, which, expanding, augmenting in force and grandeur as the significance of the work took possession of his mind, finally became an apotheosis of friendship, a message to the world.

That the Archduke appreciated Beethoven and valued his friendship is plain. He carefully preserved the letters written him by the master and dedicated to him some of his own compositions. He had as complete a library of Beethoven's works as was attainable, and was thoroughly familiar with the master's music. That Beethoven responded to this to an equal degree is not likely. He lived too abstracted a life for that. He valued this friendship as much as such a man could, considering the disparity in rank and the difference in mode of thought of the two men. In dedicating so many of his compositions to him, and in consenting to teach him for so long a period, he showed the esteem in which he held him. Probably no other person, man or woman received the deference and consideration from Beethoven, which he accorded the Archduke. The republican, socialistic Beethoven was not specially influenced by his rank; rather, it was his personality and devotion to music, which won the regard of the master and formed the bond between them.

In the composition of the mass, Beethoven was on familiar ground; the work was congenial to him. The emotions called up by the subject swayed him to such an extent that he had difficulty in keeping it within bounds. The mass was a form of music with which he had been associated from childhood. It will be remembered that he played the organ at the age of twelve years at church services, a practice which was kept up for some years. His earliest impressions on the subject of music were in this style. He was, in addition, inclined to it by temperament.

The beautiful text appealed to him strongly. It is related that when the German version of his first Mass (in C) was brought him, he quickly opened the manuscript and ran over a few pages. When he came to the Qui tollis, the tears trickled from his eyes and he was obliged to desist, saying with the deepest emotion, "Yes, that was precisely my feeling when I composed it."

His journal entries at the time of beginning work on the Mass in D show how completely the subject had taken possession of him. "To compose true religious music, consult the old chorals in use in monasteries," he wrote, which gives the clew to his frequent lapses into the ancient ecclesiastical modes, the Lydian and Dorian, in this mass, a practice for which Bach furnished a precedent. "Drop operas and everything else, write only in your own style," is another entry of this time, showing his predilection for church music.

The summer of 1818 was spent at Moedling. He was in the best of health and spirits as stated, and began the work with great energy and enthusiasm. His whole nature seemed to change, Schindler states, when he began the great work. His interest and absorption in it was extraordinary, as is shown by the sketch-books from the beginning. Enthusiasm carried him on to the consummation of a greater work than any he had yet accomplished. Hitherto, every achievement was merely a resting-place up the mountainside, the prospect acting as a spur to him to go yet higher, well knowing what Emerson finely stated, and was putting into practice at this very time, that new gifts will be supplied in proportion as we make use of those we have. *Dem Muthigen hilft Gott!* said Schiller. Beethoven seemed to have some prevision that only a few more years would be allotted him for work; when he began on the mass his inspiration was like a river that had broken its bounds. Every nerve and fibre of his being called him to his work. He was like a war-horse that scents the battle. He now abandoned himself more than ever to the impulse for creating. For the next few years he lived the abstracted life of the enthusiast to whom every-day concerns are but incidental and unimportant things, and his art the one great matter. The gigantic tone-pictures which were constantly forming themselves in his inner consciousness were of so much greater importance than the events of his external life, that the latter were dwarfed by comparison and lost their significance. He now made a greater surrender of the ties connecting him with every-day life than ever before. His industry was phenomenal, but it soon became apparent that the work would not be ready for the Installation, the date of which was set for March 20, 1820. It was in reality not completed until nearly two years after this event.

We have a good description of the master at this time by the artist Klober, who had been commissioned by a wealthy relative who was forming a gallery of famous Vienna artists, to paint a portrait of Beethoven.

"Beethoven had a very earnest look; his vivacious eyes were for the most part turned upwards, with a thoughtful and rather a gloomy expression, which I have tried to represent. His lips were closed, but the mouth was not an unkindly one. He was ready enough to expatiate on the arrogant vanity and depraved taste of the Viennese aristocracy, by whom he feels himself neglected, or at least underrated."

*   *   *   *   *

"Beethoven sat to me for nearly an hour every morning. When he saw my picture, he observed that the style of hair pleased him very much; other painters had always dressed it up as if he were going to court, not at all as he generally wore it."

*   *   *   *   *

George Alexander Fischer

"His house at Moedling was extremely simple; so, indeed, was his whole manner of life. His dress consisted of a light-blue coat with yellow buttons, white waistcoat and neckcloth, such as were then worn, but everything about him was very negligee. His complexion was florid, the skin rather pock-marked, his hair the color of blue steel, for the black was already changing to grey. His eyes were a bluish-grey and exceedingly vivacious. When his hair streamed in the breeze there was a sort of Ossian-like daemonism about him. But, when talking in a friendly way, he would assume a good-natured, gentle expression, particularly if the conversation was agreeable to him."

As we have seen, it had been a favorite project of Beethoven for years to write a mass. When he started to carry out his ideas, one course only seems to have been possible to him. This was, to project it on the principle of his Symphonies, in which the orchestra should take the commanding part in interpreting the emotional and dramatic possibilities of the text. His experience with his first mass had confirmed him in the belief that he could give the best expression to his ideas by the use of the orchestra, on account of its greater range, its mobility, the variety of its tones. The idea of making it of more importance than the voice, upset all preconceived theories on the subject. The orchestra was emphatically the tool best adapted to Beethoven's powers; he developed it into something wholly different from what it was when he found it. He put it to exquisite uses. His effects are the happiest imaginable and they are introduced with a prodigality and lavishness suggesting a reserve as of oceans from which to draw. Much of his vocal music is dominated by the orchestra.

It took a long while to make people understand that music instead of being the handmaid of poetry, whose function is merely to reflect the ideas of our spoken language, has a language of its own, which can convey ideas in itself, and that there are subtilties that can be expressed in this manner, which evade one when we come to use our coarser mode of expression. This is specially in evidence in Beethoven's later work, particularly in the mass we are now considering. Wagner frequently compares it to a symphony. In *Zukunftsmusik*, he says: "In his Great Mass Beethoven has employed the choir and orchestra almost exactly as in the symphony;" and elsewhere he cites it as being a "strictly symphonic work of the truest Beethovenian spirit."

In this work, however, he reaches out toward the infinite to a degree not attempted in the symphonies; his spirit takes a bolder flight; more of the inner nature of the artist is revealed; for the limits which bound him in the symphony were not operative in the mass. The very mode of projecting the first movement, the Kyrie, shows the splendor of the conception as it took form in his consciousness. The scheme of the movement can be summed up by the antithesis being presented of humanity, weak and sinful on the one side, and the overwhelming majesty of a just God on the other. It is a prayer for mercy, the cry of the soul in its extremity; the underlying thought being repentance. Here we have the embodiment of prayer, of supplication. A devotional feeling of the most exalted kind pervades it. The first of the three parts comprising the movement is storm and stress, a knocking on the gates, a De Profundus, an accusing conscience arraigning humanity. He works out of this vein to some extent in the second part, the Christe eleison, in which the appeal is made directly to the human element of the Godhead. In the third part, the themes of the first are again taken up, but by modulation they are made to take on a new significance, and bring peace in the end. Although the movement is cast for double chorus as regards the vocal part, the voices are given a subordinate place, the portrayal being carried on by the orchestra in true symphonic style. Notable in this movement is the rhythm. In all the storm and stress, a rhythmic motion, a systole and diastole, a surging to and fro, as of vast masses of beings in the last extremity of peril, is apparent.

To read meanings and design into the work of such a composer as Beethoven is the inevitable result of the transcendent nature of it. It was seldom that he vouchsafed any explanation of his musical intent in his compositions. Schindler, who thoroughly appreciated his genius, and who was eager for enlightenment on this phase of his art, was in the habit of drawing Beethoven out, as occasion offered, but it was always a difficult process. Simple and childlike in most matters, the master was wary and suspicious to an incredible degree when the conversation touched on the subject of his compositions. At times, however, this reserve gave way to Schindler's persistency. When he asked him about the opening bars of the C minor Symphony (the Fifth) it brought out the well-known remark, "thus fate knocks at the door." At another time, he asked him for an elucidation of the Sonatas in F minor (opus 57) and D minor (opus 29), and received the answer "read Shakespeare's Tempest," which was only half an answer. More definite is his meaning in the two Sonatas (opus 14), which represents the entreating and resisting principle in the conversation of a pair of lovers.

Men of genius seldom care to explain their utterances. "The spirit gives it to me and I write it down" is a remark attributed to Beethoven, and this stated the case sufficiently from his point of view.

Zelter, director of the Singakademie of Berlin wrote Beethoven on completion of the Mass, asking him to arrange it for voices only, as nothing but *a capella* music was permitted by the institution. To this Beethoven gave a favorable reply, saying that with some modifications the project was feasible. It, however, was not carried out.

It is significant that Beethoven gives the German direction throughout in this Mass. At the Kyrie the direction is Mit Andacht. At the soli of the Agnus Dei he writes Aengstlich, denoting great agitation or anxiety. It may have been done as a kind of protest to the Italian cult in music, which had at this period taken complete possession of the Vienna public. The more solid German music was neglected in favor of Rossini, and Beethoven felt this change of front keenly, making it the subject of remark to Rochlitz and to others.

It can readily be supposed that works like the Mass in D are not easily produced. To get his materials for it Beethoven penetrated deeply the mystery surrounding life. The ideas which he voices seem always to have existed, like other great forces in the universe; he impresses one as being the discoverer, rather than the creator of them.

Schindler, who saw much of him during these years, says of his absorption in this work: "He actually seemed possessed, especially during the composition of the Credo." It was while he was at work on this portion of the Mass, notably the great fugue, et vitam venturi (the life everlasting), that Schindler called on him one afternoon, but could not gain admission. He knew the master was at home as he could hear him stamping and shouting, singing the different parts as if mad. Finally the door was opened and Beethoven appeared. He was faint from hunger and overwork, having eaten nothing since the previous noon. His servants had, indeed, prepared some food for him the previous day, but he was too much interested in his work to think of it, and they were afraid to urge it on him, or indeed, go near him, while in the stress of composition. He had worked the previous night until overtaken by exhaustion and on awaking in the morning had at once resumed his wrk, continuing it until interrupted by

Schindler's arrival.

A work so transcendental in character as is this, calls for close and sympathetic study even to get an approximate understanding of its marvels. It is a characteristic of works of this nature, that although not easily comprehended, they are likewise not readily exhausted. Much study, many renderings only serve to bring out new values. Only by bringing to them of our best will they be revealed.

It must have been with a feeling of relief that he finally delivered a copy of the Mass complete into the Archduke's hands in March of 1822, just two years after the Installation.

Beethoven wrote the sovereigns of Russia, France, Prussia and Saxony, proposing a subscription of fifty ducats, about $115 each, for the Mass. The first acceptance came from Prussia. One of the minor officials in Vienna was commissioned by Prince von Hatzfeld, the Prussian Ambassador, to ask Beethoven if he would not prefer a royal order instead of the fifty ducats. Beethoven's reply was characteristic. Without a moment's hesitation he said with emphasis, "fifty ducats!" showing the slight value he placed on distinctions of this kind. A reply that must have gratified him very much was that received from the King of France. In his letter to him, Beethoven refers to the Mass as "*L'oeuvre le plus accompli.*" Louis XVIII, not only forwarded his acceptance (and the fifty ducats), but had also a gold medal struck off, containing his portrait on one side, and on the other, the following inscription: "*Donne par le Roi a monsieur Beethoven.*" The King of Saxony delayed his remittance for a long while, and Beethoven was greatly irritated thereby.

But little other work was undertaken during the four years he was occupied on the Mass unless we except the three grand piano sonatas, opus 109, 110 and 111, which were composed during the intervals. A mere by-product so to speak, under-taken with the object of resting his faculties jaded by the strain of the greater work, his mind notwithstanding was keyed up to a high pitch, while engaged on them. The lofty imaginings which occupied his thoughts while on the Mass are reflected in them, rendering them unapproachable as piano sonatas. The master himself, set a great value on them.

Now that the Mass was completed he began to give his attention to other works. To celebrate the opening of the rehabilitated Josephstadt theatre which occurred in the autumn of 1822, Beethoven wrote a new overture, Weihe des Hauses. He also worked over for this occasion his Ruins of Athens, written in 1812, for which the text was altered to suit the new conditions and several new numbers added. Another representation of the almost forgotten Fidelio, which was selected by Fraeulein Schroeder-Devrient for her benefit, and which was a pronounced success through the genius of this remarkable woman, led to a commission for a new opera from a Vienna manager. This was followed shortly after by a similar order from Berlin on his own terms. There had also been some talk before this about an opera on an American subject, the Founding of Pennsylvania. It was suggested by a minor poet and government official, Johann Ruprecht, whose poem, Merkenstein, Beethoven had set to music previous to 1816. In 1820 Beethoven had planned an Italian tour and had intended taking Ruprecht with him. They must have quarrelled later, as in a letter to Schindler in 1823 Beethoven refers to Ruprecht in the most abusive terms.

A commission that must have gratified Beethoven excee-dingly, but which, however, was not acted upon, was that which emanated from Breitkopf and Haertel, who sent the famous critic Friederich Rochlitz to Vienna in July, 1822, with a proposition that he write some Faust music in the style of the Egmont music. It is narrated that Beethoven received the proposition with joy, but gave only a qualified assent. There is no doubt that he would have found inspiration in the text, and that a noble work would have resulted, but he feared the nervous strain of such an undertaking. "I should enjoy it," he said to Rochlitz, "but I shudder at the thought of beginning works of such magnitude. Once engaged on them, however, I have no difficulty." His labors on the Mass aged him. In his prime on its inception, he emerged from his seclusion on completing it, infirm and broken in health. The idea of the Faust music attracted him, as it would have been strictly symphonic in character. He occasionally refers to it subsequently, but never got so far as to enter themes for it in his note-books. Wagner essayed it, but went no further than to write the overture. The subject of Faust still awaits a capable interpreter.

His next commission was a simple one, consisting of an order early in the spring of 1823 from Diabelli, composer and head of a large publishing house in Vienna, for six variations on a waltz by him (Diabelli). The dance was always a favorite musical form with Beethoven in his lighter moments, and the variation form,—capable of a degree of sprightliness, vivacity and originality in the right hands which give it an entrancing effect, to which we come again and again with pleasure, was something peculiarly his own at every stage of his artistic career. His earliest essays in composition are in this form. Variations occupy a prominent part in all his works, whether chamber-music, sonatas or symphonies. They are introduced perhaps with best effect in the works of his last years, in the Ninth Symphony, and in the last quartets.

He accepted the order with pleasure and began work on it at once on reaching his summer quarters. This was congenial work, affording him relief from the mental strain imposed on him by his labors on the Ninth Symphony, which was then under way. A price of eighty ducats ($180) was fixed by the publisher at the outset for the set, but the master enjoyed his work so much, that the six, when completed, were increased to ten, then to twenty, and twenty-five, and so on until the number grew to thirty-three. These variations are extremely elaborate and difficult, a characteristic of most of his work in these years.

Wagner never tired of exploiting the variation form in his operas, particularly in the Tetralogy. He frequently refers to Beethoven's masterly use of it. "Haydn first, Beethoven last, have conferred artistic value on this form," he says in the article on conducting; later on in the same work, he says, "the wondrous second movement of Beethoven's great C minor Sonata" (opus 111), "and the last movement of the Eroica Symphony should be grasped as an infinitely magnified Variation section." Bach also excelled in it, the Variation form being constantly met with throughout his works.

The summer of 1823 was spent at Hetzendorf, a village of which Beethoven was always fond. He had secured large and comfortable quarters in the house of a Baron Pronay, which, from Schindler's account was a fine old mansion in the centre of a large park. It suited Beethoven admirably. There was a fine view of the surrounding country from his windows, the situation was healthful, and he delighted in walking about when not at work. But he gave up this comfortable home before the summer was ended, simply on account of the extravagant politeness of his landlord, who, conscious of the value of so distinguished a tenant, always greeted him with "profound obeisances" when they met. This opera bouffe deportment though undertaken with the best of motives on the Baron's part, became so embarrassing that Beethoven finally fled to Baden with all his belongings, including the grand piano, although his rent had been paid in advance for the entire summer. Schindler assisted in this migration, joining him at five o'clock one morning.

The year 1823 in which Beethoven practically completed his life-work (with the exception of the last quartets) is the dawn of a new musical genius, versatile, accomplished, many-sided, who as performer was qualified to rank with the older master. On New-year's day of this year, Franz Liszt, who had been studying under Czerny for two years past, made his first appearance in Vienna in concert, in which he took the public by storm. Beethoven seems not to have been present, and strangely, when we reflect on his intimacy with Czerny, seems to have been unaware of the existence of this talented youth. During the autumn of this year, the elder Liszt called on Beethoven, bringing with him the young Franz. Beethoven held himself aloof at first, receiving his visitors coldly. He unbent however, on hearing the youth perform, and stooped and kissed him. During this autumn he also received a visit from Weber and young Julius Benedict, his pupil. Weber was preparing his recently completed opera Euryanthe, for a first production in Vienna. He had produced Fidelio in the foregoing spring season at Dresden, where he was officially stationed, and had made a success of it with Frau Schroeder-Devrient. Considerable correspondence must have passed between the two composers on this matter, and Weber could hardly have omitted calling when coming to Vienna, although the memory of his former strictures on Beethoven's music must have embarrassed him. Weber had stated on hearing the Seventh Symphony for the first time that Beethoven was now fit for the madhouse, and his criticisms in general had been adverse. This, however, was something which Beethoven had never objected to; more-over, time had amply vindicated him as to the symphonies, so he could afford to be generous to his youthful critic. Beethoven was genial and kindly, and the younger man was deeply impressed by the master's reception of him.

Euryanthe proved a failure and Weber called again to ask Beethoven's advice as to remodelling the work.

The libretto Melusina, which was submitted to him by Grillparzer found such favor in his eyes as to lead to its acceptance, but when he came face to face with the project, his former experience with opera was sufficient to deter him, and he abandoned the idea, giving as an excuse the inferiority of the German singers. That this was only an excuse, is plain, since only a short time afterward Mlle. Sontag was intrusted with the exceedingly difficult soprano parts of the Mass in D and the Ninth Symphony. He was hard at work on this Symphony at the time, which will serve to explain and accentuate his reluctance to again attempt operatic composition, a style of work diametrically opposed to that which had engaged his attention for many years previously. It would too, have necessitated shelving the Symphony indefinitely, and, although he needed the money which the opera would have yielded, his interest in the Symphony was paramount; he could not bring himself to abandon it. With failing powers superinduced by his excessive labors on the Mass, it was being borne in on him that he was nearing the end of his life-work. Under such circumstances the Symphony was sure to have the preference. The long cherished plans for another oratorio, and for a Requiem Mass also insistently came up for consideration, crowding out all serious intention of an opera.

The project of a Requiem Mass was of particular interest to him; it comes to the fore frequently. He mentioned it shortly after the completion of the Mass in C. Then, when his brother Karl died it is again considered. It is also mentioned on the occasion of the tragic death of Prince Kinsky, who had acted so liberally by him in the matter of the pension. It is probable that the work of writing a Requiem Mass would have proved congenial to him. He was in the right mood for it on completion of the Mass in D, and it is rather singular that he did not undertake it instead of the Symphony. Religious questions were occupying his mind more and more in these years. It must be admitted that his religion was as peculiar to himself as was his music. He affiliated with no church, although baptized as a Catholic, and brought up in that church; but the frequent appeals to the Divinity in his journals, show his belief in, and reliance on, a higher power. He formulated his own religion as did Thoreau. The man who could write, "Socrates and Jesus were patterns to me" lived a correct life in its essentials. His asceticism, his unselfishness, the sympathy which he continually showed for others, his unworldliness,—what else is this but the gist of New Testament teaching? Like a tree nourished on alien soil, which yet produces fairer and better fruit than the native ones, and becomes the parent of a new variety, this man achieved his high development of character by being a law unto himself like the anchorites of old.

CHAPTER XIV

NINTH SYMPHONY

We stand to-day before the Beethovenian Symphony as before the landmark of an entirely new period in the history of universal art, for through it there came into the world a phenomenon not even remotely approached by anything the art of any age or any people has to show us.

—WAGNER

During the period of his work on the Mass, and for some time before, Beethoven's thoughts were occupied more or less with that stupendous work, the Ninth Symphony, sketches for which began to appear already in 1813, shortly after his meeting with Goethe. That Beethoven looked up to Goethe ever after as to a spiritual mentor, studying his works, absorbing his thought, is plain. In projecting this symphony he may very well have designed it as a counterpart to Faust, as has been suggested. Actually begun in 1817, it had to be laid aside before much had been accomplished on it, in favor of the Mass in D. This gave him plenty of time to mature his conception of the work; and this ripening process, covering a period of ten years from its first inception, was one of the factors which helped him achieve his wondrous result. His work on the Mass was a good preparation for the psychological problems expounded in the Symphony.

Here is a work so interwoven into Beethoven's very life and spirit, that the mention of his name at once calls to mind the Ninth Symphony. It is the work of the seer approaching the end of his life-drama, giving with photographic clearness a resume of it. Here are revelations of the inner nature of a man who had delved deeply into the mysteries surrounding life, learning this lesson in its fullest significance, that no great spiritual height is ever attained without renunciation. The world must be left behind. Asking and getting but little from it, giving it of his best, counting as nothing its material advantages, realizing always that contact with it had for him but little joy, the separation from it was nevertheless a hard task. This mystery constantly confronted Beethoven, that, even when obeying the finer behests of his nature, peace was not readily attained thereby; often there was instead, an accession of unhappiness for the time being. Paradoxically peace was made the occasion for a struggle; it had to be wrested from life. No victory is such unless well fought for and dearly bought.

This eternal struggle with fate, this conflict forever raging in the heart, runs through all the Symphonies, but nowhere is it so strongly depicted as in this, his last. We have here in new picturing, humanity at bay, as in the recently completed Kyrie of the grand mass. The apparently uneven battle of the individual with fate,—the plight of the human being who finds himself a denizen of a world with which he is entirely out of harmony, who, wrought up to despair, finds life impossible yet fears to die,—is here portrayed in dramatic language. To Wagner the first movement pictured to him "the idea of the world in its most terrible of lights," something to recoil from. "Beethoven in the Ninth

Symphony," he says, "leads us through the torment of the world relentlessly until the ode to joy is reached."

Great souls have always taught that the only relief for this *Weltschmerz* is through the power of love; that universal love alone can transform and redeem the world. This is the central teaching of Jesus, of Buddha, of all who have the welfare of humanity at heart. It was Beethoven's solution of the problem of existence. Through this magic power, sorrows are transmuted into gifts of peace and happiness. Beethoven loved his kind. Love for humanity, pity for its misfortunes, hope for its final deliverance, largely occupied his mind. With scarcely an exception Beethoven's works end happily. Among the sketches of the last movement of the Mass in D, he makes the memorandum, "Staerke der Gesinnungen des innern Friedens. Ueber alles ... Sieg." (Strengthen the conviction of inward peace. Above all—Victory). The effect of the Choral Finale is that of an outburst of joy at deliverance, a celebration of victory. It is as if Beethoven, with prophetic eye, had been able to pierce the future and foresee a golden age for humanity, an age where altruism was to bring about cessation from strife, and where happiness was to be general. Such happiness as is here celebrated in the Ode to Joy, can indeed, only exist in the world through altruism. Pity,[B] that sentiment which allies man to the divine, comes first. From this proceeds love, and through these and by these only is happiness possible. This was the gist of Beethoven's thought. He had occupied himself much with sociological questions all his life, always taking the part of the oppressed.

[B] The German rendering *Mitleid* has a higher significance than its English equivalent. Literally it means sharing the sorrow of the afflicted one. It may be said in passing that this sentiment is the central idea in Parsifal.

George Alexander Fischer

Schindler, who was almost constantly with Beethoven at this time, tells of the difficulty the master experienced in finding a suitable way of introducing the choral part. He finally hit upon the naive device of adding words of his own in the form of a recitative, which first appears in the sketch-book as, "Let us sing the immortal Schiller's Song, 'Freude schoener Goetterfunken.'" This was afterward changed to the much better form as now appears, "O Freunde, nicht diese Toene! sondern lasst uns angenehmere anstimmen, und freudenvollere." (O friends, not these tones. Let us sing a strain more cheerful, more joyous.)

The whole character and design of the Ode to Joy will be better apprehended when it is stated that it is in reality an Ode to Freedom. With its revolutionary spirit Beethoven was entirely in accord. Already in his twenty-third year he contemplated setting it to music. Later, in the note-book of 1812, the first line of the poem appears, in connection with a scheme for an overture. It is worthy of remark that the Symphony was well under way before he decided on incorporating the Ode in it.

The Ninth Symphony was first performed in this country in 1846 in Castle Garden, by the New York Philharmonic Society, which had been organized four years previously. George Loder conducted it. When we consider the herculean efforts Wagner was obliged to make to get permission to perform it in Dresden in this selfsame year, it speaks well for "North America." Subsequent performances of it in New York by this Society are as follows:

PERFORMANCE		CONDUCTOR
Second	April 28, 1860	Theo. Eisfeld.
Third	April 29, 1865	" "
Fourth	February 1, 1868	C. Bergmann.

Fifth	April 28, 1877	Dr. L. Damrosch.
Sixth	February 12, 1881	Theo. Thomas.
Seventh	April 10, 1886	" "
Eighth	April 12, 1890	" "
Ninth	April 23, 1892	Anton Seidl.
Tenth	April 11, 1896	" "
Eleventh	April 2, 1898	Vander Stucken.
Twelfth	April 7, 1900	E. Paur.
Thirteenth	April 4, 1902	" "

It was not performed in New York during the years 1903 and 1904.

Beethoven's correspondence with Count Bruehl of the Berlin Theatre in the matter of an opera for that city, led him, owing to the apathy of the Vienna public at this time toward his works, to offer the new Symphony and the Mass for a first hearing in Berlin. At this time, and for some years previously, Rossini's music had captured the Vienna public so completely that no other was desired. That this light evanescent work should be preferred to his own, was resented by the master. He decided to offer the new works to Count Bruehl, the Italian craze not having yet penetrated Berlin. As soon as this became known however, a reaction followed, and a memorial was addressed to Beethoven by his friends, begging him to reconsider the matter, and produce the new works in Vienna, as well as write a new opera for them. The appeal was signed by thirty of the most prominent men of affairs in the city. The list of names is a noble one, each being prominently connected in some way with music. Among composers and performers may be mentioned Czerny and the Abbe Stadler. Artario & Co., Diabelli and Leidersdorf, were music publishers. Count Palfy and Sonnleithner were operatic managers, while counselor Kiesewetter and J.F. Costelli were authors of libretti and songs. The others were prominent in court circles, and their devotion to music was such as to give weight to the communication. The memorial itself is discursive to a point which taxes one's patience, but the expressions of appreciation and friendship are genuine, and must have gratified Beethoven extremely. Naturally but one outcome was probable as a result of this memorial. Shortly after receiving it, he announced to his friends that the initial performance of these works would be held in Vienna. Strangely, a difficulty at once arose, in the matter of selecting a suitable place for the performance. Had Beethoven left the management of the affair in the hands of his friends, and given his attention to securing sufficient rehearsals for the new Symphony, which finally had to be produced after being rehearsed twice only, it would have been better all around. With the vacillating disposition which characterized him in all business matters, he was not only of no aid, but so complicated matters by his indecision on every point, that the arrangements finally came to a standstill, his friends who were assisting him being at their wits' end. These were Schindler, Count Lichnowsky, and the violinist Schuppanzich. At this juncture, these old and tried friends, thinking that strategy might succeed where diplomacy had failed, hit upon the following plan to bring matters to a focus. Schindler was at this time living at Beethoven's house, and the plan decided on was to have Count Lichnowsky and Schuppanzich call there as if by accident. The conversation would naturally turn to the approaching concert and leading questions were to be asked Beethoven. His answers in these years were usually in writing. The gist of these was to be written out by one of the party, who would then carelessly, or as if in jest, ask Beethoven to sign the paper, thus committing him to a definite course. These praise-worthy intentions were carried out with so much tact and skill that Beethoven not only saw through their innocent ruse, but discovered in the whole proceeding a deep-laid plot on the part of these arch-conspirators, whereof he was to be the victim of villainy and treachery. This dawned on him shortly after the friends had taken their departure, upon which he wrote the following notes, leaving them on the piano as was his custom, for Schindler to deliver.

TO THE COUNT MORITZ VON LICHNOWSKY,—
I despise these artifices, visit me no more. Academy (the concert) will not take place.

BEETHOVEN

TO M. SCHINDLER,—
Do not come near me again until I send for you. No Academy.

BEETHOVEN

TO M. SCHUPPANZICH,—
Do not visit me again. No concert.

BEETHOVEN

From the above it will readily be seen, as Schindler plaintively asserts, that the office of friend to Beethoven was no sinecure. But he appreciated the advantage of living in the reflected glory of the great master, and such tact as he possessed was brought to bear, to continue the relations of friend, counsellor and general factotum, which were maintained to the end. Beethoven at times spoke slightingly in his letters of his humble follower, but there is no doubt that Schindler was of great service to him, and that this was appreciated by the master is equally true. Schindler did not deliver the letters just quoted, and the affair did not sever the relations of the parties concerned.

Beethoven's contention all along was for an advance in price of admission to the concert, owing to the heavy expense for theatre hire, copying, etc. As the works to be performed had not yet been published, it was necessary to copy out the separate parts for the members of the orchestra and chorus,—an immense task. The manager objected to any advance in prices, and insisted also that the concert be held on a subscription night—a good arrangement for the patrons of the theatre who would thus have free admission, but a bad one for the master. He finally had to submit, however. "After these six weeks' squabbling," he writes to Schindler toward the end of April, "I feel absolutely boiled, stewed and roasted," a state of mind brought about by his conflict with copyists, managers and performers.

The concert which took place on May 7, 1824, was the occasion for great enthusiasm. The programme consisted of the Overture Weihe des Hauses, as well as the Kyrie, Credo and Agnus Dei of the Mass in D, and the Ninth Symphony. The solo parts were taken by Madame Sontag and Fraeulein Unger, who protested more than once at the unsingable nature of some of the parts in the Choral Finale when practising them at Beethoven's house.

The applause from the very beginning was phenomenal. The people became vociferous on seeing him, and this enthusiasm was continued throughout the evening. At the close of the performance the demonstrations became, if possible, more forcible than before, owing, perhaps, to the fact that Beethoven maintained his former position, facing the orchestra and with his back to the audience, as if unaware of the applause. At last Fraeulein Unger turned him about so that he could see the demonstrations of the audience. The picture is presented of excited masses of people carried away by the emotions of the moment, rending the air with boisterous applause, and in the midst this great one, unresponsive to the homage showered on him, unconscious, seeing visions, perhaps planning a Tenth Symphony.

Beethoven's deafness was not total. He was no doubt able to

hear some of this extraordinary applause, and, in any event, must have known that it would be forthcoming. He had probably become wearied with it all, and let his thoughts go far afield. The utter vanity of this kind of thing must often occur to great minds at such a time. These frenzied people by their very actions showed their inability to comprehend his work, and could not confer honor in this manner.

But the enthusiasm of the audience had the practical effect of leading the manager to make an offer to Beethoven for another concert, guaranteeing him five hundred florins ($250). It was held on May 23, at noon. On this occasion all of the Mass but the Kyrie was omitted, some Italian music being substituted. The house was only half filled at the second concert and the management lost money. Beethoven's apprehensions as to the profits from the first concert were well founded. He made less than two hundred dollars from the undertaking, and was so disappointed with this pitiful result after all the work of preparation, that he refused to eat any supper, and would not go to bed, but remained on a couch with his clothes on for the night. When he learned that the management lost eight hundred florins on the occasion of the second concert, it was with difficulty that he could be prevailed on to accept the amount guaranteed him. It is not likely that this reluctance was owing to any consideration for the manager, but rather to umbrage at the course of things in general. His temper was not improved by these disappointments, and he even charged Schindler with having conspired with the manager to cheat him. This led to a rupture between the two of several months' duration. Beethoven at length called on Schindler and apologized for the offence, begging him to forget it, upon which the old relations were restored.

Notwithstanding that Beethoven had personally solicited the attendance of the members of the Imperial family, and had promises from some of them, not one came, the Emperor's box being the only empty space in the theatre. The slight was no doubt intentional, and affords the last instance of which there is record, of the lifelong contest waged between Beethoven and the court. He was usually the aggressor, making it impossible for the Imperial family to favor him, or even to show him much attention. They could not have been insensible to the historical importance of having in their midst such a man; they must have had the prescience to know that Beethoven's achievements, if furthered by them, would place them in the lime-light for the admiration of future ages; but they were thwarted by the man himself, who went out of his way more than once, most unjustifiably, to offend them.

There is a letter from Count Dietrichstein, court chamberlain, on the subject of a mass which Beethoven was invited to write for the Emperor, which is unintentionally humorous. In it, all sorts of suggestions are made as to the style of the music, the length of the mass (it being enjoined on him that the Emperor did not like long church services) and other like stipulations. Beethoven's remarks in answer to this letter are not recorded, but the mass was not written. Here was a case where kingly prerogative did not avail.

Simultaneously with the appearance in the sketch-books of motives for the Ninth Symphony, another is projected, as was the case when composing his previous ones, which generally appeared in pairs, as already noted. A wealth of ideas flowed in on him while engaged on any great work, much of which, when not available for the one, could be utilized on the other. While working on the Mass in D, he had in mind composing another mass, as is evidenced by the following memorandum in the sketches of the Agnus Dei: "Das Kyrie in der neuen Messe bloss mit blasenden Instrumenten und Orgel." (The Kyrie in the new Mass only with wind instruments and organ.) The new Symphony was to be religious in character, and was projected on a broader scale even than the Ninth. A memorandum on the subject of the Tenth Symphony appears in the sketch-books of the latter part of the year 1818. It is as follows: "The orchestra (violins, etc.) to be increased tenfold, for the last movements, the voices to enter one by one. Or the Adagio to be in some manner repeated in the last movements. In the Allegro, a Bacchic festival."[C] His labors, however, on the Mass and Ninth Symphony had so exhausted him that no strength was left for this great work, and no part of it was even drafted. Later he thought to substitute a shorter work, something which would not have taxed him so much physically. He then makes the memorandum, "also instead of a new Symphony, an overture on Bach." Sehr fugirt (greatly fugued.)

[C] Nottebohm's *Zweite Beethoveniana*.

Now that the concerts were over and summer approaching, Beethoven's thoughts turned to the country. A comfortable house was secured for him at Schoenbrun on the bank of the river, but his stay here was short. A bridge near the house made it possible to obtain a good view of the master, and it soon got to be the custom for people to station themselves on it and watch for his appearance. He stood the ordeal for three weeks, and then fled to his beloved Baden, where he appears to have been safe from such annoyances.

CHAPTER XV

CAPACITY FOR FRIENDSHIP

Genius lives essentially alone. It is too rare to find its like with ease, and too different from the rest of men to be their companion.

—SCHOPENHAUER

For many years Beethoven had not been on speaking terms with the friend of his youth, Stephen von Breuning. The year 1815, which had cost him his brother Karl, also deprived him of Stephen's friendship. Two versions are given as to the cause of the quarrel which estranged them. One is that Stephen had warned him not to trust his brother Karl in money matters. Another, and probably the correct one, is that Stephen endeavored to dissuade the master from adopting the young Karl in event of his brother's death. In either case Von Breuning acted entirely in Beethoven's interest without considering the possible consequences to himself; his disinterestedness was poorly rewarded however. Beethoven was bound by every obligation of friendship to him, but, with his usual want of tact, told his brother just what Stephen had said. Naturally Karl resented this interference in their family affairs, and succeeded in inflaming his brother's mind against Von Breuning. The estrangement resulted. Karl died shortly after, and a mistaken sense of loyalty toward his dead brother helped to keep alive Beethoven's anger against his former friend. There is no record of his having so much as mentioned the latter's name in the following ten years, although he and Von Breuning lived in the same city and had many friends in common.

As time passed, and one after another of Beethoven's friends were lost to him—through death or otherwise—his thoughts no doubt often reverted to this old friend. It must often have occurred to him that Breuning's companionship would be more enjoyable than that of some of the friends of these years. An accidental meeting with him on the bastion one evening in August of 1825, happily led to a reconciliation. Beethoven's eyes were at last opened to the injustice done Von Breuning, upon which he wrote him a letter, so imbued with penitence, so fraught with the desire of obliterating his past unkindness, so filled with yearning and tenderness, that it must have compensated Stephen for all the pain of the past years.

Accompanying the letter was his portrait painted many years before. The letter has been frequently published. It is so characteristic of the man that it can hardly be omitted:

"Behind this portrait, dear, good Stephen, may all be forever buried which has for so long kept us apart. I have torn your heart I know. The agitation that you must constantly have noticed in me has punished me enough. It was not malice that prompted my behavior toward you. No! I should then be no longer worthy of your friendship. I was led to doubt you by people who were unworthy of you and of me. My portrait has long ago been intended for you. You know that I had always intended it for some one. To whom could I give it so with warmest love as to you, true, faithful, noble Stephen.

Forgive me for causing you suffering. My own sufferings have equaled yours. It was not until after our separation that I realized how dear you are and always will be to my heart."

All this in English sounds cold and stunted when compared with the fire of the original. Beethoven never spared himself when making amends for past misconduct.

From this time on the name of Von Breuning appears again in his letters and he found much comfort in intercourse with his family. He was always a welcome guest at Breuning's house. A friendship was soon inaugurated between the master and Stephen's son, a bright lad of twelve years. He nicknamed him Ariel, when sending him on errands, probably with reference to his agility.

Such incidents as the quarrels with Breuning, his dismissal of Schindler, Schuppanzich, and Count Lichnowsky during the preliminary work of the testimonial concert, his suspicions of his friends at the second concert when he invited them to a dinner, and then charged them with an attempt to defraud him,—these at first glance, especially if considered apart, lead to the conclusion that Beethoven was not intended for friendship. This was not the case however. His deafness and preoccupation with his work, led him to keep aloof to some extent from others, but it is undeniable that he greatly valued this sentiment and actively fostered it. Perhaps, like Thoreau, he expected too much from it, and could find no one to respond to the measure of his anticipations. He was probably disappointed one way or another, with every friend that came to him, but to the end kept alive his faith in humankind, and managed always to maintain intimate and friendly relations with one or more persons. There is no interval from his twentieth year up to his death, of which this cannot be said. He was essentially gregarious and recognized the need of friendship. That he was unlike his fellow human beings—essentially different—he knew. He often sought to bridge these differences, in order to make friendly intercourse with others possible.

Among the friends of this period may be mentioned Huettenbrenner, Schubert's friend. Schubert himself would have prized Beethoven's friendship in the highest degree, but he was too modest to bring it about. The junior by twenty years, and in Beethoven's lifetime unknown to fame, it devolved on him to take the initiative in this matter. A meeting could easily have been arranged as both dined at the same restaurant, and Huettenbrenner could have managed to bring them together. Beethoven was generally approachable when not at work, and was always well disposed toward young musicians of talent, but the habitually modest estimate which Schubert placed on himself, coupled with the regard amounting to reverence which he entertained for Beethoven, was sufficient to deter the younger man. He indeed attempted a meeting in 1822, but the result was a fiasco owing to his extreme diffidence. Having composed some variations on a French air (opus 10) he desired to dedicate them to Beethoven and prevailed on Diabelli to arrange a meeting, as well as call with him on the master, since he feared to go alone. Beethoven's demeanor toward him was genial and friendly. When Schubert attempted conversation the master handed him a pencil and paper. He was too nervous to write in reply, but managed to produce his composition, which Beethoven examined with some appearance of interest. The master finally came upon some incorrect harmonization (Schubert had never received a proper technical training) and in mild terms called the young composer's attention to it. This so disconcerted him that he fled to the street, regardless of consequences. The incident is related by Schindler, but is called into question by Kreissle, who wrote an exhaustive biography of Schubert. Kreissle says that Beethoven was not at home when Schubert called.

Excessive diffidence was not the distinguishing trait of another young man, Karl Holz, who had ingratiated himself into the master's favor in these years. Holz had a post under government, was of good social position, possessed fine conversational powers, and was an all-round entertaining and agreeable person. He was a musician of first-rate attainments, a member of the Schuppanzich Quartet, and occasionally acted as director of the Concert Spirituel of Vienna.

Holz's gayety and light-heartedness helped to dispel the melancholy which had become habitual with Beethoven at this time. He had the discernment to see that such an atmosphere was unsuited to a young man of Karl's temperament, and may very well have encouraged Holz's visits on his nephew's account. The situation had its defects however, as Holz's convivial habits were communicated to Beethoven, who was led at times to drink more wine than was good for him. Beethoven, in one of his letters to his nephew, reproached him with being a thorough Viennese, to which the young man retorted in kind, alluding to the master's friendship with Holz. This was before the reconciliation with Von Breuning had been effected. After that event he saw him less frequently. The young man however, retained his hold on the master's regard and maintained the footing of an intimate friend for the remainder of his life. Flashes of the old humor constantly appear in his letters to Holz, which, though tinctured somewhat with coarseness, make pleasanter reading than his remark to Fanny del Rio—"My life is of no worth to myself. I only wish to live for the boy's sake." Holz took him out of this mood.

In the last year of his life Beethoven, at Holz's request appointed him his biographer as follows:

VIENNA, *Aug. 30, 1826.*

I am happy to give my friend, Karl Holz, the testimonial he desires, namely,—that I consider him well qualified to write my biography if indeed, I may presume to think this will be desired. I place the utmost confidence in his faithfully transmitting to posterity what I have imparted to him for this purpose.

LUDWIG VAN BEETHOVEN.

Holz, however, was not equal to the requirements, and this duty was relegated to Schindler.

A curious change affected Beethoven in his later years on the subject of money. It was not avarice, that "good old-gentlemanly vice" of Byron's which influenced him, but it resembled it at times. With his nephew as the inciting cause, money, to which he had hitherto been indifferent, now assumed a new value to him. This is evidenced by absurd economies (alternated it is true by occasional extravagances), which are a feature of this time. The diminution of his pension, the nature of the compositions of these years from which for the most part no money was available, the cessation of his teaching (Von Frimmel mentions a pupil, Hirsch, who had a few lessons from him in 1817, which was probably the last of Beethoven's sporadic attempts in this direction, as his deafness must have made teaching extremely difficult), were all factors which rendered money a scarce article with him. In the same ratio in which his income had been diminished, his expenses were increased by the maintenance and education of his nephew, which in large part was borne by Beethoven.

This new estimate of the value of money was strengthened by the conviction that Karl would never do anything for

George Alexander Fischer

himself, and that provision must be made for his future. To this must be attributed his solicitude for money which is constantly in evidence in his letters to his friends, as well as to his publishers, in which latter the disposition to drive a good bargain comes to the fore now for the first time. His letters to Ries are full of the subject of making money. "Waere ich nicht noch immer der arme Beethoven," he says with unconscious humor, in one of the letters. "If I could but get to London, what would I not write for the Philharmonic Society. If it please God to restore my health, which is already improved, I may yet avail myself of the several propositions made me, not only from Europe, but even North America, and thus my finances might again prosper."

His naive reference to this country[D] refers to the offer made him by the Haendel and Haydn Society of Boston for an oratorio, the text of which was to be furnished by them. His work on the Ninth Symphony prevented him from accepting it, but it is something that will always redound to the credit of the society. That the critical faculty should, already at that time, have been sufficiently well developed in this country as to lead to such a commission, augurs well for its future art-history. While one portion were engaged in subduing the wilderness, fighting Indians, extending the frontier, others were already reaching out for the highest and best in art and literature.[E] It is a pleasant reflection that this country is no longer the terra incognita in musical matters that it was in Beethoven's time. The ready recognition extended Wagner from the first here, has, no doubt, helped to bring this about.

[D] When writing this letter Beethoven could have had no prevision that in this aboriginal North America, in a little village called Natick, there was then living a five-year-old boy, answering to the name of Alexander W. Thayer, who was eventually to furnish a biography of the master, so painstaking, exact and voluminous, that it is unique in its class. The Beethoven biography was Thayer's life-work, to which he gladly sacrificed his means as well, and was then only brought down to the year 1816. Thayer's name will always be associated with that of Beethoven, it is such a record-making work. It is published only in German at this writing (1904), but an English translation is promised on completion of the second edition, one volume of which has appeared in 1902. Mr. Thayer died in 1897.

[E] That Beethoven's genius had at an early date impressed itself on the minds of Americans, was commented on by Margaret Fuller in 1841. She says:

"It is observable as an earnest of the great future which opens for this country, that such a genius (Beethoven) is so easily and so much appreciated here, by those who have not gone through the steps that prepared the way for him in Europe. He is felt because he expressed in full tones the thoughts that lie at the heart of our own existence, though we have not found means to stammer them as yet."

Meanwhile Ries, in London, was making active propaganda for him, with the result that an offer had come to him from Charles Neate asking him to come to London with a symphony and a concerto for the Philharmonic Society. Neate was a great admirer of Beethoven. He had spent eight months in Vienna some years previously, and the two became good friends during this sojourn. Three hundred guineas, and a benefit concert in which five hundred pounds more was to be guaranteed him, was the inducement held out for coming. This large sum tempted him strongly, placing him, so to speak, between two fires. The character of his nephew was such that he could not be left behind, while his education would be interrupted if he took him along. His entries in his journal show with what dread and apprehension he faced the ordeal of going among strangers. The project never would have been considered but for his desire to provide for Karl's future. The journey was never undertaken, but the project was never abandoned. It occupied his thoughts even in his last illness.

The scores of the Mass and Symphony were sold to Messrs. Schott of Mayence, one thousand florins having been obtained for the Mass, and six hundred for the Symphony. This put him in easy circumstances for a while, although the money question was a source of anxiety to him, more or less, for the remainder of his life. The ten thousand florins invested in Bank of Austria shares in 1815 was almost intact. He had drawn on it once or twice when matters had come to an extremity with him, but to touch it in any other case seemed to him like betraying a trust, since it had been set aside as a provision for his nephew. Just before the testimonial concert, he was at times absolutely without funds, his housekeeper being occasionally required to advance money from her savings to tide him over until a windfall should happen. The proceeds from the seven subscriptions to the Mass in D, amounting to three hundred and fifty ducats (about eight hundred dollars) helped him out to some extent, and something must have been coming in all the while from his previous publications. With good management there would have been sufficient for a man of his simple requirements, but in nothing was he so deficient as in business ability, or the faculty of looking after his worldly concerns. He was probably cheated right and left in his household matters.

CHAPTER XVI

THE DAY'S TRIALS

Those who are furthest removed from us really believe that we are constituted just like themselves, for they understand exactly so much of us as we have in common with them, but they do not know how little, how infinitesimally little this is.

—WAGNER: *Letter to Liszt*

Beethoven was in no sense a hero to his servants. In their eyes he was not the great artist, whose achievement was to go ringing down the ages; he was simply a crank or madman, who did not know his own mind half the time, from whom abuse was as likely to be predicated as gratuities, who could be ridiculed, neglected, circumvented with impunity. When the dereliction became glaring enough to arrest his attention, he would deliver himself of a volley of abuse which sometimes had to be made good by presents of money. At other times, he desired nothing so much as to be left alone.

That he found the world a more difficult problem than ever in these later years, goes without saying. "Have you been patient with every one to-day?" he asks himself in one of the note-books of this period, indicating the dawn of a perception that fate is too much for him, that it can be defied no longer, but rather must be propitiated. Had he answered his question, it would no doubt have been in the negative; but this attitude, so new to him, is significant. It comes up also in his letters to Zmeskall, in which he speaks of his patience in enduring the insolence of a butler, who had been sent him by Zmeskall.

Complaints about servants appear frequently in his correspondence. Peppe, the "elephant-footed," and Nanny, who seems to have had a particular faculty for making trouble, are specially in evidence. "I have endured much from N. (Nanny) to-day," he writes in a letter to his good friend Madame Streicher, who was very helpful to him in his domestic matters. On one occasion, when her conduct became unbearable, he threw books at her head. Strangely, this method of disciplining the refractory Nanny produced better results than could have been expected. He reports soon after to Madame Streicher, "Miss Nanny is a changed creature since I threw the half dozen books at her head. Possibly, by chance some of their contents may have entered her brain, or her bad heart. At all events we now have a repentant deceiver."

In another letter of this time he writes to the same lady, "Yesterday morning the devilry began again, but I made short work of it, and threw the heavy settle at B (another servant), after which we had peace for the remainder of the day." "Come Friday or Sunday," he writes Holz. "Better come on Friday, as Satanas in the kitchen is more endurable on that day." This advice to come on Friday when purposing to dine with him, is repeated in a subsequent letter to Holz. "If I could but rid myself of these *canaille*," he writes to another person, when complaining of the hostility and insolence of his servants.

That his own mode of life helped largely to bring about this state of things, did not make it any easier to bear. As stated, system was out of the question in this household. There was no regular time for meals, often no meals were thought of by the master while occupied with his work. When hungry, if nothing were forthcoming at home, he sought a restaurant. Careless in general as regards his food, abstemious to a degree in this respect, he was particular only on one matter, his coffee. He delighted in making it himself, often counting the beans that were required for each cup.

"My house resembles very much a shipwreck" is a remark attributed to him by Nohl. Even under favoring conditions, discipline was not to be expected, but matters were further complicated by Karl's mother, who made a practice of bribing the servants to get information about the young man. There is no doubt her influence tended to increase the discomfort and disorder that would have existed in any event. "Some devils of people have again played me such a trick that it is almost impossible for me to mix with human beings any more," he said in a letter to Madame Streicher, which remark Mr. Kalischer (*Neue Beethovenbriefe*, Berlin, 1902), attributes to intrigues against him by his sister-in-law.

To illustrate the slight regard his servants had for Beethoven and their absolute ignorance of the value of his work, an incident related by Schindler about the loss of the manuscript of the Kyrie of the Mass in D is in point. On reaching Doebling in 1821 on his annual summer migration, he missed this work and the most diligent search failed to bring it to light. Finally the cook produced it; she had used the separate sheets for wrapping kitchen utensils. Some of them were torn, but no part was lost. No copy had yet been made, and its loss would have been irreparable.

The difficulties which he experienced with the world in

general existed with his copyists and engravers to an exaggerated degree as may be supposed, since proofreading was a matter on which he was extremely particular. He was apt to make unreasonable demands on them, not understanding human nature. He wanted them to work quickly and accurately and they were very often slow and careless; they tried his patience more than his servants did. A little deftness on his part when in contact with them, would have made things easier all around. As it was, they received little consideration from him, and gave but little in return. He was so deeply interested in his compositions that he frequently recalled them after they were in the engraver's hands, in order to make alterations and additions. The Sonata, opus 111 was withdrawn twice, after the engraver had actually begun work on it. It had been sold to Diabelli, who finally refused to return it again, as the engraver's work in each case was thrown away. This called out a sarcastic letter from Beethoven to Schindler, in which he refers to Diabelli as an arch-churl (*Erzflegel*), and threatens him (Diabelli), if he is not more amenable.

"I have passed the forenoon to-day, and all yesterday afternoon in correcting these two pieces and am actually hoarse with stamping and swearing," he wrote the copyist in reference to the A minor Quartet. Elsewhere he complains about the carelessness of the publishers of his earlier quartets, which are "full of mistakes and errata great and small. They swarm like fish in the sea, innumerable."

When referring to the testimonial concert, allusion was made to the enormous labor involved in copying out all the parts required for the occasion, in which over one hundred persons participated. To examine and correct each copy before placing it in the hands of the performers was in itself no slight task. The labor of making the seven subscription copies of the Mass, was probably a still greater one. In these days of cheap publications, one can hardly form an estimate of what it really meant. Many months elapsed after the Mass was completed, before a clean copy could be gotten for the Archduke even.

No doubt the copyists often misunderstood the master's instructions, always given in writing in his later years. He was so careless with his handwriting that some of his letters are undecipherable in part, to this day. Schindler, with good common-sense made a practice of transcribing Beethoven's words on the back of any letter received from him before filing it away. The master's extraordinary carefulness in proof-reading has already been mentioned. This was to him a matter of the utmost importance, second to none. Press of work, illness even, was not allowed to interfere with the careful revision of his work.

He might write about patience in his note book, but it was exercised very little when dealing with his copyists. There were times in this connection in which the situation became so strained that they refused to work for him. In one such instance a man, Wolanck by name, returned the manuscript which the master had sent him, writing him at the same time an impertinent letter. This copyist was evidently of a literary turn, with a talent for satire. He begins by begging to be permitted to express his gratitude for the honor which Beethoven has done him in being allowed to drudge for him, but states that he wants no more of it. He then proceeds to philosophize on the situation, saying that the dissonances which have marked their intercourse in the past have been regarded by him with amused toleration. "Are there not" asks this Junius, "in the ideal world of tones many dissonances? Why should these not also exist in the actual world?" In conclusion he ventures the opinion that if Mozart or Haydn had served as copyist for Beethoven, a fate similar to his own would have befallen them.

A wild Berserker rage took possession of Beethoven on receipt of this letter which he appeased characteristically by writing all sorts of sarcastic comments over the sheet, and by inventing compound invectives to suit the case. He heavily criss-crossed the whole letter, and across it in heavy lines wrote, "Dummer Kerl" (foolish fellow), "Eselhafter Kerl" (asinine fellow), "Schreibsudler" (slovenly writer). On the edges at the right: "Mozart and Haydn you will do the honor not to mention"; at the left: "It was decided yesterday, and even before, that you were not to write for me any more." On another spot he writes: "correct your blunders that occur through your fatuity, presumption, ignorance and foolishness." (Unwissenheit, Uebermuth, Eigenduenkel, und Dummheit). "That will become you better than to try to teach me."

In better vein is a letter from Beethoven to the copyist Rampel, who had worked for him during a period of many years. He had Beethoven's favor more than any other copyist, on account of a peculiar faculty he possessed for deciphering the master's handwriting.

Bestes Ramperl,—

Komme um morgen frueh. Gehe aber zum Teufel mit deinem Gnaediger Herr. Gott allein kann nur gnaedig geheissen werden.

BEST RAMPEL,—

You can come to-morrow morning, but go to the devil with your "Gracious Sir," (Gnaediger Herr). God alone should be addressed as "Gracious Lord."

This letter was published in the Beethoven number of *Die Musik*, February, 1902.

CHAPTER XVII

LAST QUARTETS

Every extraordinary man has a certain mission, which he is called upon to accomplish. If he has fulfilled it he is no longer needed on earth, in the same form, and Providence uses him for something else. But as everything here below happens in a natural way, the daemons keep tripping him up until he falls at last. Thus it was with Napoleon, and many others. Mozart died in his thirty-sixth year. Raphael at the same age. Byron a little older. But all these had perfectly fulfilled their missions, and it was time for them to depart that others might still have something to do in a world made to last a long while.

—GOETHE, *Conversations with Eckermann*

In the midst of these ironies of fate, this satyr-play of the nether forces with the master, in which he occupies at times so undignified a position, it is gratifying to note that the artist-life goes on apace. In the last quartets which now come up for consideration, the labors of the tone-poet are brought to a close.

The quartet was a favorite musical form with the master.

George Alexander Fischer

Here the more intimate side of his nature is revealed. A more personal relation is established between composer and audience than is the case in the other forms in which he worked. As we have seen, the quartet, in the time of which we write, was universally in use at informal gatherings for the delectation of friends in the privacy of the home, and was not intended for concert use. The stateliness which characterizes the large symphonic forms is absent in chamber-music, but it has qualities of its own which we value as much.

The last quartets owe their existence to Prince Galitzin, a Russian nobleman, who had spent some time in Vienna in 1805, and became acquainted with Beethoven at the house of the Russian Ambassador, Count Rasoumowsky, for whom it will be remembered Beethoven composed three quartets, opus 59. In November of 1822 the Prince wrote Beethoven in the most flattering terms, asking him to compose three quartets at his own price, which were to be dedicated to him. The master accepted the commission gladly, fixing the modest sum of one hundred and fifty ducats (about $330) for the three, reserving, however, the right to sell the quartets to a publisher. Prince Galitzin was then living in state in St. Petersburg. His wife was a fine pianist, he himself a first-rate performer on the cello. They occupied a prominent position in the musical life of the city. The Prince was one of the original subscribers to the Mass in D, and has the credit of having brought about the first complete performance of this colossal work ever given.

When we consider the enormous expense of this under-taking, the copying of the many parts, as well as the sums paid for soloists, chorus and orchestra, most of which was probably borne by the Prince, and reflect that this is only an instance among many of his extravagant mode of living, it is not surprising to find that he became financially embarrassed, and was unable to carry out in full his obligation to Beethoven as regards paying for these works.

The Oratorio, "The Victory of the Cross," which had already been begun, was laid aside in favor of the quartets; it was never resumed. Notwithstanding his enthusiasm, work on the new commission made but slow progress. Ill health and preoccupation in his nephew's concerns took up much of his attention. Occasional sketches were made, but it was more than a year and a half before the first one was actually begun. It was outlined at Baden in the autumn of 1824, and finished on his return to Vienna. Mention is made of this quartet by the master in an interesting letter to Messrs. Schott of Mayence, who had bought the mass and symphony, and had also purchased the quartet, paying fifty ducats for it. Cordial relations had been established with these gentlemen, dating from the time of selling them the two great works just mentioned. Some of Beethoven's best letters are those written to his publishers. An extract from the letter above referred to follows:

"The quartet you shall also receive by the middle of October. Overburdened by work, and suffering from bad health, I really have some claim on the indulgence of others. I am here on account of my health, or rather to the want of it, although I already feel better.

"Apollo and the Muses do not yet intend me to become the prey of the bony scytheman, as I have yet much to do for you, and much to bequeath, which my spirit dictates and calls on me to complete before I depart hence for the Elysian Fields; I feel as if I had written scarcely more than a few notes."

The initial performance of the first of the Galitzin Quartets took place in the spring of 1825. Beethoven regarded the event as a momentous occurrence and required the four performers, Schuppanzich, Weiss, Linke and Holz, to sign a compact, each to "pledge his honor to do his best to distinguish himself and vie with the other in zeal."

The quartets once begun were carried on with ardor in the midst of most distressing occurrences, chief of which were ill health and its twin demon, poverty, as well as the waywardness of his nephew, all of which tended to draw him to the spiritual life. The character of Beethoven's work changed from the period of the Mass in D. An altered condition, an altogether new, different strain is apparent thenceforth. The deeply religious, mystical character of the first movement of the Ninth Symphony can be attributed to his previous absorption on the Mass. He worked out of this vein somewhat in the other movements as not being adapted to the uses for which the symphony is designed, but it reappears again in the quartets to the extent of dominating them.

The one in B Flat, opus 130, completes the three for Prince Galitzin. Of the Cavatina of this quartet, Holz is authority for saying that Beethoven composed it with tears, and confessed that never before had his own music made such an impression on him; that even the repetition of it always cost him tears. In this movement Beethoven used the word *Beklemmt* (*Beklommen*) (oppressed, anxious) at a point where it modulates into another key. His loneliness, superinduced by his life of celibacy, by his deafness, his disappointment in his nephew, all had the effect of separating him from the world. The spiritual side of his nature, always active, had been brought into new life during his work on the Mass, as we have seen. It was never thenceforth allowed to fall into abeyance, but was developed in direct ratio with his withdrawal from the world. An atavism from some remote Aryan ancestry inclined him, as in the case of so many Germans, to mysticism and the occult. It was a condition which had its compensations. That there were periods when he saw visions may be conjectured by the character of the last quartets. When they were written, Beethoven was in the shadow of death, on the border-land of the other world, and from that proximity he relates his experience. These works receive the reverence of all musicians for their spirituality, their mysticism, their psychological qualities. They are the revelations of the seer, awe-inspiring mementos of states and conditions of mind which transcend the experiences of ordinary life. In these last impassioned utterances of the master, we find a strain holier, more profound, different from anything which the art of music has yet produced.

The Cavatina on its first performance, on March 21, 1826, was received with indifference, and the finale, which was an exceedingly long and difficult fugue, fared even worse. Self-sufficient as Beethoven was on all matters connected with the working out of his musical thoughts, he coincided for once with his friends and the publisher on the matter of the fugue. He wrote a new finale for the quartet, and published the fugue separately as opus 133. Joseph Boehm, the noted violinist, then in his twenty-eighth year, rehearsed this fugue under Beethoven's direction, and often played the violin part subsequently.

The great C sharp minor Quartet opus 131, is the next one to claim our attention. Beethoven characterized it as a piece of work worthy of him. This colossal work was one which Wagner continually held up for the commendation of mankind. It occupies among quartets a position analogous to that of the Ninth Symphony in its own class. The summer of 1826 in which it was composed, was a period fraught with momentous occurrences to the master, chief of which was the attempted suicide of his nephew. The circumstances which led up to this catastrophe can be briefly narrated. Beethoven had been disappointed in any and every plan formed for the future of the young man. He at first looked for great things from him; by gradual stages his expectations were so modified that at last he began to fear that he would never be able to provide for his own maintenance.

The musical education of the young man had first engaged the master's attention, in the hope that some of the family talent might have been transmitted to him. When it became plain that nothing could be achieved by him in a musical career, he was entered at the university of Vienna with a view of making a scholar of him. Here he was unable to keep up with his studies, owing to inattention. He failed to pass his examination and left the school in consequence. Literature being closed to him, he entered the Polytechnic school, intending to fit himself for business life, but failed here also. That Karl's conduct caused the master much anxiety appears in his letters to him. In some of them he entreats him to do better, in others he upbraids him. Both lines of reasoning seem to have been equally obnoxious to this careless, indifferent young man, who objected to being taken to task for his misdeeds, and hated "rows" and "scenes" with his uncle. When he failed the second time he was at his wits' end in dread of his uncle's reproaches. Many a stormy scene had occurred between them during the two preceding years. So violent had these become, that the master was on one occasion requested to find another apartment on account of the complaints that came from other occupants of the house. It may very well be that Beethoven expected too much from this carelessly reared youth, whose mother lost no opportunity of embittering him against the master. The young man probably never seriously contemplated suicide, but wanted to give his uncle a scare. By working on his fears he reasoned that he would be able to have his own way for a long while to come. He threatened suicide, and the day following this threat actually went so far as to shoot himself. He was not severely injured, but the attempt on his life rendered him amenable to the laws of his country, and a short confinement in the government hospital followed.

Beethoven was greatly agitated on learning of the rash act. He had some difficulty in finding him, as the young man had left his quarters and went to another part of the city before carrying out his threat. With the aid of friends he was finally located and an affecting scene followed in which the master loaded him with kindness, treating him very much as that other prodigal son was treated by his father.

Beethoven's personal intervention with the magistrate eased the situation for the nephew. Two very interesting letters from the master in this connection were published some years ago in the Neuen Freien Presse of Vienna, and are included in Herr Kalischer's Beethovenbriefe published in Berlin in 1902. The following one shows Beethoven's ethical character in strong light:

To the Magistrate Czapka:

DEAR SIR:

Hofrath von Breuning and I have carefully considered what is best to be done. We think for the time being no other course is practicable than that Karl should remain with me a few days (during the interval until he can enter the military service). His language is still excitable under the impression that I would reprimand him since he was capable of making an attempt on his life. He has, however, shown himself quite affectionate toward me. Be assured that to me fallen humanity is still holy. A warning from you would probably have good results. It would do no harm to let him know that unobserved he will be watched while with me. Accept my highest esteem for yourself, and consider me as one who loves his kind, who desires only good wherever possible.

Yours respectfully,
BEETHOVEN

In accordance with the English custom of putting the fool of the family into the army, Stephen von Breuning had hit upon the plan of a military career for Karl since all others seemed closed to him. Von Breuning, who always had a faculty of being of service to Beethoven, was a counsellor in the war-office. He urged on Beethoven the feasibility of procuring an appointment for Karl in the army, and interested his superior, Field-marshal Lieutenant von Stutterheim, in the matter. Beethoven was not greatly in favor of a military career for the young man. "Uebrigens bin ich gar nicht fuer den Militaerstandt," he says in a letter to Holz of September 9, when the subject was first broached. He opposed it for a while, but finally bowed to the inevitable.

Toward the end of October, and before the negotiations in regard to the army appointment were concluded, the young man was released from the hospital, and placed under the control of the master, with the injunction that he be removed from Vienna at once. At this juncture brother Johann placed his country house at Gneixendorf at the disposal of the master and nephew, and thither the two repaired, the elder, stricken, bowed with grief; the youth, sullen and indifferent. The master had never entered Johann's house since the summer of 1812, when he had tried so ineffectually, as noted in a previous chapter, to break up the relations existing between the pair while the lady was as yet only the housekeeper. It must have been with great reluctance that he considered visiting him at all. The sacrifice, if such there was, was made in the interest of Karl; where this young scapegrace was concerned, the master was generally willing to sink his own preferences. The situation must have been embarrassing for all concerned, less so in reality for the master than for the others. Absorbed in the composition of the new finale, and also in the finishing up of the great C sharp minor Quartet, he was for the most part oblivious to anything unusual in his surroundings. Johann's wife, with the policy of her class, bore no resentment, or at least showed none outwardly. A pleasant room on the ground floor was fitted up for him, but the welcome must have been a cold one at best.

No doubt the Gutsbesitzer took much pleasure in showing off his possessions to the brother whom he knew had little esteem for him at heart. He paraded his own importance in the neighborhood, taking the composer on business visits to prominent people. On these occasions he would not usually introduce his brother, treating him as a kind of appendage. The master, deep in the thought of creative work, was, no doubt, to a great extent unconscious of this sordidness. At all events he gave no sign. But he contributed very little to the social well-being of the family. Two aims only seem to have occupied his mind at this time: the welfare of his nephew, and the carrying to completion of a few great works already sketched or begun. These included a Tenth Symphony, (for the Philharmonic Society of London), the Oratorio, The Victory of the Cross, for the Vienna Gesellschaft der Musikfreunde, music to Goethe's Faust, which latter he must have been in good mood for,—as well as an overture on Bach. "I hope yet," he writes from Johann's home, "to bring some great works into the world, and then like an old child, to close my earthly career somewhere among good people." He worked with feverish haste in the latter years of his life, whenever his health permitted, even abandoning his books in favor of his work. Failing health prevented him from forcing it ahead as in former years, but he worked up to the limit of his powers.

His habits while composing have been referred to in a previous chapter, namely, that he was in the habit of singing, stamping, gesticulating, while under the spell of his inspiration. This kind of thing was new to the maid who looked after his room, and she managed to extract amusement from it. Beethoven finally discovered her laughing at him, and forthwith bundled her out of the room, giving orders that no female would be admitted again. One of the men about the place, Michael Kren, was then engaged, who performed his duties faithfully, and helped materially to establish a more comfortable existence for the sick, helpless man. He has narrated circumstantially the master's mode of life while at Gneixendorf. He was up and at work at half-past five, beating time with hands and feet, singing, humming. This went on until breakfast time, half-past seven. This meal over he would hurry out of doors, (the weather was fine that particular autumn) spending the morning going about the fields, note-book in hand, his mind intent on his musical thoughts, occasionally singing or calling out, going now slowly, then very fast, at times stopping still to write out his ideas. This would go on until noon, when he would return to the house for dinner. This was served at half-past twelve, after which he would go to his room for about two hours, then again to the fields until sunset. He was never out in the evening as night air was considered bad for him. Supper was served at half-past seven. His evenings were spent in his room, and at ten o'clock he went to bed.

This simple, regular life, with the healthful country air, should have restored Beethoven's health in some measure could it have been continued longer. His letters from here indicate that he expected some improvement in this respect. Had not some untoward circumstances intervened, the master's life might have been spared long enough to enable him to carry to completion the list of works outlined above.

That Johann had an ulterior object in asking his brother to visit him is quite probable. The growing fame of the composer and the ever-increasing value of his copyrights was well known to him. He had made money in his dealings between composer and publisher in the past, and could have made still more had he possessed his brother's confidence in a greater degree. His cupidity however, prevented him from keeping up for long even the semblance of kindness or hospitality. Fuel was so scantily provided the sick guest that he suffered from cold, and he was told that a charge would be made for the room. Other circumstances may have contributed to bring about a climax. At all events the situation became so unpleasant that he suddenly decided to return to Vienna.

George Alexander Fischer

CHAPTER XVIII

IN THE SHADOWS

As a day well spent gives joyful sleep,
So does a life well spent give joyful death.

—LEONARDO DA VINCI

The C sharp minor Quartet and the one in F, opus 135, which rounds out this wonderful series, were all but completed before leaving Vienna on the visit to Johann. That there was some polishing still to be done on the latter is apparent from the fact that it has the superscription in the master's handwriting, "Gneixendorf am 30 Oktober 1826." The finale has these curious sentences: "Der schwergefasste Entschluss. Muss es sein? Es muss sein." Question and answer turn on the subject of paying his room rent according to Schindler, the dialogue being a reminiscence of previous times. Beethoven often made some discussion when his rent was demanded, either from the desire to extract some sport from the situation, or from fear of being cheated. It often had to be demonstrated to him by the aid of an almanac that the time was up and the money really due.

The only work begun and completed by the master while at

Gneixendorf was the new finale, which replaced the long fugue of the B flat Quartet. It proved to be his last work. The series of unpleasant events referred to in the last chapter ensued, and, without considering consequences, he returned to Vienna.

It is not likely that Johann or his wife exerted themselves much to keep him longer. They intended spending the winter in Vienna themselves, and were probably relieved to have the visit ended so that they could make their preparations for the journey. With his usual impatience, he must needs take the first conveyance which was to be had. Johann had a closed carriage, but would not let him have it, and the journey was made in a light open wagon. December had arrived and the weather, which had been fine all the fall, was now bad. He was insufficiently clothed for the two days' drive in such weather. He contracted inflammation of the lungs on the way, and reached his quarters in the house of the Black Spaniards, a very sick man.

This house, his last earthly abiding-place, had been his home for the past year. It was a disused monastery, which had been established in 1633 by the daughter of Philip III of Spain on taking up her residence in Vienna after her marriage. The original building was destroyed in one of the wars of that turbulent time, but was rebuilt at the end of the seventeenth century. The building was demolished in 1904. It was situated on the glacis, in a part of the city where Beethoven had lived much of the time since coming to Vienna.

The fates seem to have been against him from the beginning of his journey. His sleeping-room was an enormous one on the second floor, which, with two small anterooms, composed the apartment. The facilities for heating a room of that size, in those times must have been wholly inadequate. Several days elapsed before a physician could be found to attend him. He had quarrelled with two of his former physicians and each refused his aid. Finally, a professor from the medical college, a Dr. Wawruch, was summoned, who took the case in hand. Schindler states that it was several days before he or any of the master's friends knew of his arrival in Vienna, and leaves the inference that he was unattended during this interval except by his nephew. When they learned of his return, Schindler and Stephen von Breuning were unremitting in their attentions.

As Beethoven had taken a violent prejudice against Dr. Wawruch, another physician, Dr. Malfatti, was engaged, who acted in conjunction with the former. The treatment was now changed, large quantities of iced punch being administered, probably with the view of relieving the congestion of the stomach. This mode of treatment exactly suited the sick man, a result which was probably foreseen by the astute Dr. Malfatti, who had prescribed for Beethoven during previous illnesses and knew his patient's idiosyncrasies. Beethoven's childlike simplicity is illustrated in the difference of his demeanor toward his two physicians. He always had a warm welcome for the one who had administered the iced punch, remembering no doubt its immediately alleviating and beneficial results, but Dr. Wawruch fared poorly at his hands, especially when he was in a bad humor. On more than one occasion when the latter appeared the patient turned his face to the wall with the remark, "Ach der Esel."

Everything possible was now done to add to his comfort. Two servants were engaged to attend him. His friends cheered him by their visits. Huemmel called, bringing his young pupil Ferdinand Hiller. Some of Schubert's songs were brought him, probably by Huettenbrenner. They consisted of Die Junge Nonne, Der Taucher, the Ossian songs, Die Buergschaft. Schindler states they awakened the master's surprise and delight, eliciting from him the remark,

"Truly, Schubert has the divine fire."

Beethoven was so eager for work that he attempted composition again in the intervals of his illness, but his strength was not sufficient to enable him to go on with it. Hitherto his one resource in every difficulty had been his work. The injunction of Saint-Simon, to lead during the whole of the vigorous portion of manhood the most original and active life possible, had been perforce carried out by him. Now that his one resource, work, failed him, he was bereft. He sought to pass the time by reading, and began with Kenilworth in a German translation, but soon threw it down saying: "The man writes only for money."

The volatile Holz did not fail him in his need, but manifested his friendship by many kind acts. His former publishers the Haslingers, Tobias and Karl, as well as Diabelli, called occasionally. The Archduke at Olmuetz could hardly have been expected to come, especially as a fatal termination was not for some time considered probable. We hear nothing of Czerny, of Schuppanzich, of Linke, or of Zmeskall, which to say the least, is singular. Schindler's omission of these names, however, has no particular significance; he wrote many years after the event, and forgot or omitted the mention of circumstances of greater importance than this. It is not like what we know of the character of Czerny, or Zmeskall, to neglect Beethoven in his extremity. The master's old friend, Stumpf, of London, sent him a splendid edition of Haendel's works in forty volumes, with which he occupied himself a good deal. They afforded him much enjoyment.

Anxiety on account of money, so prevalent all through these latter years, was increased by his enforced abstinence from work. What he chiefly desired now was sufficient ready money to carry him through, so that he would not have to break into the little hoard put by for Karl many years before.

At this juncture the Philharmonic Society of London sent him one hundred pounds, being an advance payment on account of a concert they intended giving for his benefit. The initiative in this matter was taken by Beethoven himself, and it is safe to say that nothing that was done for him during this period was so appreciated, or gave him so much pleasure, as this act of kindness from the Society. The money reached him about ten days after an operation had been performed on him for the relief of the dropsical accumulations incidental to his liver trouble. Four such operations had been found necessary during this illness. They were at best only palliative. His joy on receiving the letter and money from London was such that the wound, not yet healed, opened, and a great discharge followed. A letter of thanks was sent to the Society, dictated by the master, but he was too weak even to sign it.

Schindler relates that Beethoven on nearing middle-age, was wont to indulge himself in day-dreams of a prosperous future, in which he could have sufficient means to enable him to live in comfort, keep his carriage like brother Johann, and have leisure for the refinements of life. This illusion, maintained by most workers, no doubt brightened his prosaic, solitary life. Pity that he could not have realized it in some measure: after the heat and burden of the day, in which he had so well acquitted himself, it would seem fitting, had he had an evening of life such as was vouchsafed Wagner, with opportunity for completing his life-work in peace and contentment.

One result achieved by the master as a consequence of his visit to Gneixendorf would have afforded him great satisfaction could he have known it. The matter of making suitable provision for Karl in event of his own death had lain on his conscience for some time before this visit, as already stated. While there, he begged his brother Johann to make a will in Karl's favor, which eventually came to pass.

The army appointment, of which mention has been made, became an established fact early in December, and the young man soon after left Vienna to join his regiment. Beethoven never saw him again. He by this time concurred with his friends in the opinion that the discipline of military life might be beneficial to him, and was resigned to the separation.

The great C sharp minor Quartet is indelibly associated with Karl, through its dedication to Baron von Stutterheim, through whom the appointment came. The decision to dedicate this work to the Baron, was arrived at only two weeks before the master's death. The work had been for some time in the hands of the publishers, Messrs. Schott of Mayence. Beethoven, finally becoming aware that no more works could be produced by him, and wishing to reward the Baron in the only way possible, dictated an urgent letter to Messrs. Schott on the subject. "The Quartet," he said, "must be dedicated to Field-marshal von Stutterheim, to whom I am under great obligations. Should the first dedication by any possibility be already engraved, I beg of you, on every account, to make this alteration. I will gladly pay any extra expense connected with it."

The last Quartet, opus 135, is dedicated to Johann Wolfmayer, a merchant of Vienna with whom he had much friendly intercourse. Wolfmayer showed his interest in the master's work in many ways. It may be mentioned that he offered him a sum equal to several hundreds of dollars to carry out his project of writing a Requiem Mass. "Write to Stumpf and Smart," he said to Schindler a few days before his death, when already too weak to speak above a whisper. His consideration for others was paramount even in the face of approaching death.

Notwithstanding the hopeful tone which characterized the letters written during his last illness, there were times when he knew that he was making a losing fight. Already on January 3, a month after his return from Gneixendorf, he wrote a letter to his attorney, Dr. Bach, in the form of a will, in which as may be supposed, his nephew is his sole heir. No conditions were imposed on the young man, who, had the will remained in this form, might have squandered the entire amount. (The estate netted $5000). This was pointed out to Beethoven by his counsellor, Dr. Bach, and also Von Breuning, who urged on him the necessity of adding a codicil to the will, in which the principal would be tied up for life, leaving only the income available. This he resisted to within a few days before the end, but finally gave in, and, not without great difficulty, wrote with his own hand a codicil, consisting of but three lines, in which the income only was to be enjoyed by the nephew, the principal to revert to his natural or testamentary heirs, after Karl's death. Breuning, true to his sense of duty, not satisfied with having gained his point, endeavored, at the risk of antagonizing the master, to change the words "natural or testamentary heirs," to "legitimate heirs." Beethoven was obdurate on the point, however, saying, "the one term is as good as the other." Von Breuning, good faithful friend that he was, survived Beethoven but one year.

Schindler dwells on the perfect tranquillity of Beethoven in the face of approaching death. "Plaudite amici, comoedia finita est," he said on the day when the codicil was written. On the following day at noon, he received the last rites of the church. The event was no doubt a solemn one. Soon after, the death-struggle began, and continued without interruption for two days. Huettenbrenner was a faithful attendant during these last days. His friend Schubert also called, at least once, and, it is said, was recognized by Beethoven, although he was unable to speak to him.

The nervous strain on his friends in witnessing this struggle between life and death, in which but the one issue was possible, must have been great. It was, no doubt, a relief to Schindler and Von Breuning to leave the master in Huettenbrenner's charge on the afternoon of the 26th of March, and go to Wahring in order to secure a burial-place. While on this necessary errand, a terrific storm arose, which prevented their return until night. Meanwhile, Huettenbrenner, left alone with the master, endeavored to ease his position by sustaining his head, holding it up with his right arm. His breathing had been growing perceptibly weaker, carrying the conviction that the end was near. The storm was of unusual severity, covering the glacis with snow and sleet. The situation of the building was such that it was exposed to the full fury of the tempest. No sign was given by the master that he was conscious of this commotion of the elements. With the subsidence of the storm at dusk, the watcher was startled by a flash of lightning, which illumined everything. This was succeeded by a terrific peal of thunder which penetrated even Beethoven's ears. Startled into consciousness by the unusual event, the dying man suddenly raised his head from Huettenbrenner's embrace, threw out his right arm with the fist doubled, remained in this position a moment as if in defiance, and fell back dead.

The two friends returned some hours after all was over. The master died at a quarter before six o'clock on the evening of March 26, 1826. He was in his fifty-seventh year.

The funeral took place on March 29 at 3 P.M. from the church of the Minorites and was attended by many of the most prominent people of the city. Eight musicians bore the coffin from the house to the church, while thirty-two torch-bearers followed it, among the number being Czerny and Schubert. This was followed by a choir of sixteen male singers, and four trombones, which alternated in singing and playing. The music consisted of two equali composed by Beethoven many years before, arranged for this occasion by Seyfried, to the words of the *Miserere* and *Amplius*.

Notwithstanding the immense concourse of people assembled at the obsequies, estimated at twenty thousand, there was but one relative to occupy the position of mourner, and that was Johann.

On April 3, Mozart's Requiem was sung at the church of the Augustines, and shortly thereafter, Cherubini's Requiem was sung for him at the Karlskirche.

The magnificence of his funeral, when compared with his simple mode of life, calls to mind the great contrasts which he was always producing in his music. Equally great contrasts had always come up in his life. Living in the proudest most exclusive and bigoted monarchy in Europe, at a time when feudal authority had not yet been entirely abolished, he held himself to be as good or better than Emperor or Cardinal. On receiving a request one morning from the Empress of Austria to call on her, he sent back word that he would be busy all that day, but would endeavor to call on the following day. There is no record of his having gone at all. His unjustifiable conduct toward the Imperial family, while at Toeplitz with Goethe, has been touched on in a previous chapter. Frimmel states that something similar occurred at Baden, but does not give his authority. Beethoven arraigned the Judiciary, even when writing conciliatory letters to the judges. In his letters to the different magistrates during the litigation over his nephew, he is often satirical and sarcastic in spite of himself. His criticisms of other judges, his references to the manner in which justice is administered in Austria, illustrate his temerity and independence. His scorn of the King of Saxony, on account of being dilatory in paying the subscription for the Grand

Mass, was pronounced. He alludes to him as "the poor Dresdener" in his letters, and he even went so far as to talk about suing him when the payment was still longer withheld.[F] All this from a man who at times did not have a decent coat to wear, or a second pair of shoes; who sometimes accepted advances from his housekeeper for the necessaries of life. His life was so simple and circumscribed that he never saw the ocean, or a snow-covered mountain, although living within sight of the foothills of the Alps. He never returned to his native city though living not a great distance from it.

[F] Kalischer. *Neue Beethovenbriefe.* Berlin, 1902.

The immediate cause of death, as demonstrated by the post-mortem held the day after his decease, was cirrhosis of the liver, the dropsy, of which Schindler makes such frequent mention, being an outcome of, and connected with, the liver trouble. The organ showed every indication of chronic disease. It was greatly shrunken, its very texture being changed into a hard substance. That alcoholism is the commonest cause of cirrhosis is well known, but in Beethoven's case some other cause for the disease must be found. He was in the habit of taking wine with his meals, a practice so common in Vienna at that time that not to have done so would have been regarded as an eccentricity, but he never indulged in it to excess, except possibly on a few occasions when in the company of Holz. It can hardly be brought about by the use of wines, but is produced by the inordinate use of spirituous liquors, something for which Beethoven did not care. Cirrhosis was probably the cause of his father's death, as he was a confirmed inebriate; but this cannot be connected with the cirrhosis of the son; the disease is not transmissible.

Beethoven's deafness probably began with a "cold in the

George Alexander Fischer

head" which was neglected. The inflammatory process then extended to the Eustachian tubes. When it reached this point it was considered out of the reach of treatment in his time, and for long after. Even in our own time, in the light of advanced medical science, such a condition is serious and is not always amenable to treatment, some impairment of the hearing frequently occurring even with the best of care and under conditions precluding the thought of a congenital tendency. The difficulty as revealed by the post-mortem, lay in a thickening of the membrane of the Eustachian tubes. The office of these tubes is to supply air to the cavity on the inner side of the drum-membrane, known as the middle ear. As is well known, a passage exists from the outer ear to the drum. The Eustachian tubes connect the middle ear with the upper portion of the throat from whence the air supply to the middle ear is obtained. We cannot imagine a drum to be such unless there is air on both sides of the membrane. Exhaust the air of an ordinary drum, and its resonance would be gone. A similar condition obtained with Beethoven. With the closure of the Eustachian tubes the air supply to the middle ear was cut off; the air in the cavity finally became absorbed, and a retraction and thickening of the drum-membrane with consequent inability to transmit sound vibrations followed.

The hypothesis of heredity, sometimes brought forward to account for his deafness, would have more weight had the lesion shown itself in the case of either of his other brothers. As it is, there is no hint to be found of even a tendency to deafness in any other of the Beethovens, whether Johann, Karl, or the nephew. In any event a congenital tendency of this kind would have been more likely to develop itself in Karl, the weakling, than in the sturdy Ludwig.

The master's known impulsiveness and carelessness in matters connected with the preservation of his health, lead to the conclusion that he himself contributed much to his deafness. He was fond of pure air outside, but sometimes had for a sleeping room an alcove wholly without ventilation, so dark that he had to dress in another room. We hear much of his practice of taking brisk walks on the ramparts or in the suburbs, in the intervals of his work. There is at least one instance on record,—there were probably many such cases,—of his coming in after a walk, overheated, perspiring, and seating himself before an open window in a draught. Another hygienic measure which he abused was his custom of frequently bathing his head in cold water while at work, probably to counteract the excessive circulation of the blood in the head brought about by his brain-work. A chilling of the body, particularly in the neck and the back of the head when overheated is a frequent cause of inflammation of the middle ear. Von Frimmel calls attention to the dust-storms which are a feature of Vienna. They were probably worse in Beethoven's time than now, as but little attention was paid to hygienic measures in those days. This no doubt aggravated the trouble.

CHAPTER XIX

LIFE'S PURPORT

Das Grenzenlose braust um mich. Weit hinaus glaenzt mir
Raum und Zeit. Wohlan! Wohlauf! altes Herz.

—FRIEDERICH NIETZSCHE

Beethoven's life in its devotion to the attainment of a single
end, the perfection of his art, affords an object lesson, which
cannot fail to encourage and stimulate every one engaged in
creative work of any kind. His earnestness and industry is the
key-note to his achievement. He worked harder than any
composer we have any record of, with the possible exception
of Wagner. If we consider how the compositions improved
in his hands, while being worked over, as is shown by the
sketch-books, a simple process of reasoning will convince
the reader that any man's work, in any line, can be improved
by adopting the same methods. Beethoven's own words in
this connection are, "the boundary does not yet exist, of
which it can be said to talent cooperating with industry,
'Thus far shalt thou go and no farther.'" The more he worked
over his compositions the better they became. When he
required a theme for a particular purpose, if the right thought
did not at once come to mind, his practice was to write as

near it as possible. By the time this was done an improvement would suggest itself. He would then write it again, and before the ink was dry, would start at it yet again, each effort bringing him nearer the goal, and this progress was the incentive that led him to continue until the idea he was reaching for became a reality. His intuitive faculties were highly developed, and he had Goethe's "heavenly gift" of imagination, but this would have been as nothing without his power of concentration. All his abilities were focused on his art. He made everything else subservient to the one idea of attaining perfection in it. He succeeded too, by giving his genius free play, by allowing his individuality to shape itself in accordance with its own laws. The circumstances of his life favored this action. Responsible to no one for years before reaching maturity, he was nowhere hampered or repressed as might have been the case had he had a home life. Strong characters are best left alone to work out their own development. It is only the weak ones that have to be supported. He met every demand that his art made on him. It was only by a complete surrender, by a concentration of all his forces into one channel, that he attained his results. By losing the world, he gained it. The great ones in every age, in every art or calling,—those who attained to saintship,— seers,—prophets,—all went this road.

He had absolute confidence in his judgment. He seldom considered what his audience would like. The best that was in him was what he gave to the world. He knew its value, and if others could not understand it, he knew the time would come when it would be appreciated. In art as in religion, faith is a necessary preliminary to all great achievements.

In going so far beyond us, in pushing the art to the limit of its possibilities, Beethoven has made portions of his work inaccessible to the large body of people who look upon music as an art for enjoyment only. The same kind of problem that is presented to this generation in the works of his last years, confronted his contemporaries in those of his middle life, which were as far beyond the comprehension of his own generation as the more abstruse works of his last years are beyond the ability of the present. To a future age, seemingly, has been relegated, as an heritage of the past, the best fruit of Beethoven's genius. When the Mass in D and the last Quartets can be heard frequently, a new era in the art will have been inaugurated.

It would be a mistake to suppose that Beethoven was a pessimist, or a misanthrope. Placed here to live and suffer, not knowing why it should be so, he yet teaches that relentless fate cannot prevail against those who make a good fight. "I did not wish to find when I came to die that I had not lived," said Thoreau, paraphrasing from Voltaire, (most men die without having lived). "I did not wish to live what was not life, living is so dear." Beethoven's idea of the purport of life was similar. He believed, and put his theory into practice, that each man has within himself the potentialities with which he shapes his own destiny. Fate and Destiny are verities that have to be faced, but they do not have all their own way with us. Each of us has the power to control his destiny to some extent. By willing it so the tendency is toward betterment. Always the highest powers are on our side. Life, after all, is worth while. This was the gist of his philosophy. He sought to establish an optimistic view of life, with the object of making the problem easier to solve.

Fichte, in his work "Ueber das Wesen des Gelehrten", gives the literary man the place of priest in the world, continually unfolding the Godlike to man. This was also Beethoven's aim. Haydn charged him with being an atheist, but his works as well as his life refute this charge. The Kyrie and the Agnus Dei of the Mass in D, could never have been produced had he been other than a devout, religious man. In his journals he continually addresses the Godhead. Outwardly, however, he gave no sign. "Religion and general-bass," he said once, with a touch of humor, "are in themselves two inscrutable things (*abgeschlossene Dinge*) about which one should not argue."

He was solicitous that his nephew should receive proper religious instruction, and made this a point in his letters to the magistrates while the lawsuit over him was in progress. After giving his ideas as to the proper education of the young man, in which French, Greek, music and drawing take a prominent place, he adds, "I have found a holy father who has undertaken to instruct him in his duties as a Christian, as well as a man, for only on this foundation can we bring up genuine people." Again, "It is for his soul's welfare that I am concerned. Wealth can be achieved, but morality must early in life be inoculated" (*eingeimpft*). He saw the necessity of religion; that it has been called forth through the consciousness of utter helplessness in the individual. Man is encompassed on all sides by inexorable laws, produced and perpetuated by a power beyond and outside the comprehension. The expression of the religious sentiment is his effort at propitiation, and is his one resource. This is the point of view on which Beethoven projected the grand mass. It is what governed his life.

An inner pressure led him to choose a life of self-abnegation and rectitude. He saw through and over and beyond the illusions and allurements of the senses, and so was enabled to live entirely in harmony with the moral order of the world, in an age, and among a people, largely given over to the pursuit of pleasure.

A long life is generally considered the best gift which the Fates have to bestow. In the summary of a man's life it is usually treated of as implying special virtues in the subject. But a long life in itself is as nothing in comparison to the quality of the life that is lived. It is by achievement only that its value can be determined.

WAGNER'S INDEBTEDNESS TO BEETHOVEN

FOREWORD

Beethoven, in Wagner's estimation, is a landmark in music, just as Shakespeare is in literature, as Jesus or Buddha in religion. He is the central figure; all others are but radii emanating from him. To Beethoven was it given to express clearly what the others could but dimly perceive. The relation of men like Bach or Haendel toward Beethoven, Wagner held to be analogous to that of the prophets toward Jesus, namely, one of expectancy. The art reached its culmination in Beethoven. This is Wagner's summary of the significance of Beethoven's work, and he proclaimed it continually, from the housetops. It was in some sort a religious exercise to him to make propaganda for the master to whom he felt himself so deeply indebted. The burden of his utterances on the subject of the musician's art is, "A greater than I exists. It is Beethoven."

Chiefly, perhaps, of the philosopher and the poet must we needs feel that if any genius reaches out into an interpenetrating spiritual world, *theirs* must do so.— F.W.H. MYERS,

Human Personality, Chapter on Genius

In art the best of all is too spiritual to be given directly to

George Alexander Fischer

the senses; it must be born in the imagination of the beholder, although begotten by the work of art.— SCHOPENHAUER.

Wagner's achievement can be attributed, in part, to a certain quality of intellectual receptivity, by virtue of which he was enabled to appropriate to himself the genius of two of his predecessors for whom he had a special affinity. His epoch-making work was rendered possible through Shakespeare and Beethoven, who served him as models all his life.

Every great achievement is referable to some preceding one often quite as great but more obscure. No man stands alone in his deed. The doer of every great work has been helped thereto by his predecessors working the same soil. The greater the performance, the more prominently this comes out sometimes, as in the case of Shakespeare whose indebtedness to Christopher Marlowe and others will at once come to mind.

To Beethoven and to Shakespeare, Wagner paid tribute on all occasions. Especially is this true in his relation to Beethoven, to whom he readily yields the palm in the realm of music. In the eight volumes of his *Gesammelte Schriften*, no single fact stands out more clearly than his recognition of Beethoven as his chief, his master, from whom proceeds all wisdom and knowledge and truth. One can hardly read any of Wagner's prose writings without seeing how readily he falls into the place of disciple of Beethoven. "I knew no other pleasure," he says in A Pilgrimage to Beethoven, "than to plunge so deeply into his genius that at last I fancied myself become a portion thereof." The Pilgrimage, though an imaginative work, is the medium he employed to give utterance to his regard for Beethoven. His letters to musical friends, to Liszt, to Fischer, especially those to Ulig, are filled with praise of the older master. In a letter to

Meyerbeer, in 1887, he states how he came to be a musician. "A passionate admiration of Beethoven impelled me to this step." The only one who was good enough in Wagner's eyes to be compared with Beethoven, was Shakespeare. These two names are frequently brought into juxtaposition in his works. No musician is worthy of comparison with his demigod. "Mozart died when he was just piercing into the mystery. Beethoven was the first to enter in," he says in his Sketches. As if even this praise were too great, he severely criticises Mozart's operas and symphonies elsewhere.

The deferential attitude which Wagner assumes toward Beethoven is not accorded any other musician. Consciously or not, when he talks about other musicians (except Bach) he, for the most part, assumes the role of censor. But Beethoven comes in for unstinted praise. "It is impossible," he says, "to discuss the essential nature of Beethoven's music without at once falling into the tone of rhapsody."

Wagner seems hardly to have been able, when writing about music, to refrain from mention of Beethoven, he is so full of the subject. It has a bearing on every important event in his life. At the ceremonies attending the laying of the foundation-stone of the Festival Play House at Bayreuth, the Ninth Symphony was performed, and in a little speech he says: "I wish to see the Ninth Symphony regarded as the foundation-stone of my own artistic structure." In "Religion and Art" we find these words: "to whom the unspeakable bliss has been vouchsafed of taking one of the last four symphonies of Beethoven into his heart and soul."

Many enthusiasts have worked in Wagner's cause from Liszt down, but none have equalled Wagner in this respect—in enthusiasm for *his* master. He pays tribute to Beethoven in all conceivable places. He first heard of him when told of his death. His first acquaintance with Beethoven's music was a year after the master's death, on his arrival at Leipzig at the Gewandhaus concerts. Wagner was then in his sixteenth year. "Its impression on me was overpowering," he says. "The music to his Egmont so inspired me that I determined not to allow my own completed tragedy to be launched until provided with such like music. Without the slightest diffidence I believed that I could write this needful music." He had up to this time no special leaning toward music. He had not previously entertained a thought of it as a career, but his first hearing of Beethoven's music decided him to adopt it, such was the kinship between these two minds. Through Beethoven he discovered that "music," to use his own words, "is a new language in which that which is boundless can express itself with a certainty impossible to be misunderstood."[G]

[G] Thoreau, in 1840, expressed himself similarly. We quote from the recently published Service. "Music is a language, a mother tongue, a more mellifluous and articulate language than words, in comparison with which speech is recent and temporary. There is as much music in the world as virtue. In a world of peace and love music would be the universal language and men greet each other in the fields in such accents as a Beethoven now utters at rare intervals at a distance."

The episode made a turning-point in his life. Hitherto his whole mind and thought had been placed on literature, the drama in particular, as a career. Through Beethoven he first learned what a power music possesses in the portrayal of the emotions and passions. He had, as he says, an intimate love and knowledge of Mozart without apparently being much influenced thereby. Up to this time Shakespeare had been his archetype. Now, with a fine discriminating intelligence, marvellous in a youth of sixteen, Beethoven is to be included in this hero-worship, and is eventually to supplant his former ideal. "It was Beethoven who opened up the boundless faculty of instrumental music for expressing elemental storm and stress," he says in the "Art-Work of the Future," and elsewhere in the same article, "the deed of the one and only Shakespeare, which made of him a universal man, a very god, is yet but the kindred deed of the solitary Beethoven, who found the language of the artist-manhood of the future."

Wagner's criticisms on music are admirable. Here he expresses his thoughts as plainly as in his compositions. His disquisitions on music as an art and on Beethoven in particular, are always lucid and forcible. He may be misty in his philosophical speculations, but when he speaks on music it is in the authoritative tone of the master, familiar with every phase of his subject. He always contributes something of value, and his thoughts are an illumination.

Had Wagner never written a line of music, had he elected to be a literary man, a poet, a dramatist, philosopher, his fame to-day would still be world-wide. Had he confined his genius into this one channel of literary expression, as was his original intention, with his mental equipment, and a Napoleonic ambition that balked at nothing, the product would have been as original and extraordinary, we may be sure, as is his art-product in music. Wagner, the musician, is so commanding a figure that the literary man is obscured; but when we consider the magnitude of his literary achievement, the dramas Tannhaeuser, Lohengrin, Flying Dutchman, Tristan, Parsifal, the stupendous Ring of the Nibelung, the essays on music, philosophy, criticism and sociology, and reflect that it is, so to speak, a by-product, it becomes apparent that, had he made literature his chief aim in life, the result would have been notable in the annals of the century.

Wagner seriously contemplated writing a biography of

George Alexander Fischer

Beethoven at one time, and devoted several months to collecting materials for it. But his finances were still in bad shape, and he was unable to undertake it without an order from some publisher, who would have been required to advance money. He was unable to find such a party, and the project was abandoned, most unfortunately, as he would have made a valuable contribution to the subject. The short biographical sketch he wrote on Beethoven on the centenary anniversary of the master's birth, shows marvellous insight, especially in relation to the critical and analytical parts of it. This work, instinct with worship of the master, is a product of Wagner's mature years. Here, as in his earliest utterances on Beethoven, he is the disciple glad to do homage to his master.

"A century may pass," said Schopenhauer in a letter to the publishers of the (English) Foreign Review and Continental Miscellany, offering to translate Kant for them, in response to a wish he had seen expressed in their journal that England might ere long have a translation of Kant, "a century may pass ere there shall again meet in the same head so much Kantian Philosophy, with so much English, as happen to dwell together in mine." Likewise centuries may elapse before another such musician will appear possessing the literary ability, critical faculty, ardor and enthusiasm that Wagner had for this work.

There is an affinity between them in which mind speaks to mind. When writing on Bach's influence on Beethoven, he says:[H] "If Haydn passed as teacher of the youth, for the mightily unfolding art-life of the man, our great Sebastian Bach became his leader. Bach's wonder-work became his Bible; in it he read, and clean forgot that world of clangor heard no longer." This describes Wagner's own spiritual relationship to Beethoven, and the exaltation that must have been his on reading the symphonies, the Mass in D, the overtures. He exhausts himself in praise of each. He makes the Third Leonore Overture of as much account as the entire opera; he continually refers to the Egmont and the Coriolanus Overtures, and says that in the latter and in the Third Leonore, Beethoven stands alone and beyond all imitation.

[H] Mr. Ellis's translation.

An evidence of Wagner's overpowering genius exists in the originality and unique character of his work, while giving himself up so unreservedly to this spiritual guidance. The two, however, were quite unlike in many respects. Neither could have done the work of the other. Beethoven, almost a failure in operatic composition, undertook it no more after one trial, while Wagner was irresistibly drawn to this style from the beginning. He felt that with Beethoven the last word had been said in pure instrumental music, while his literary talents also served to draw him into this field of operatic composition where they could find their proper outlet. With that unerring poetic sense which guided him in the selection of his subjects, he always has the romantic element to the fore. The atmosphere of romanticism which invests all his works, is what gives them much of their value. Through the force and purity of his literary instinct, he was enabled to select topics of supreme interest, so that his imagination was kept at white heat while composing. His originality and absolute confidence in himself prevented him from following Beethoven to any marked extent. He was forced to hew out a new path for himself. He was, however, not averse to occasionally taking a hint from him when it would serve his purpose. It is the prerogative of genius to take its material wherever it can be found. "Plato," said Emerson, "plays sad havoc with our originalities." Beethoven's influence is plainly discernible in the preludes and overtures of the Wagner dramas, which are symphonic throughout. The frequent use Wagner makes of the trombones, when he wishes to be particularly impressive, recalls Beethoven. Each had a high opinion of the trombone where solemnity was required, and made constant use of it. Beethoven applied it with peculiar effect in the Benedictus of the Mass in D, and in the Ninth Symphony, which is paralleled by Wagner's use of it in Parsifal, and in the Funeral march in Siegfried. The extraordinary uses to which he puts the pedal-point, as well as the variation form, are instances which show the influence of the older master.

When, however, he takes an idea from Beethoven, he improves on it, broadening and amplifying it, in general putting it to a better use than it was where he found it. A great dramatic work admits of fuller and longer treatment of an idea than is possible in the other forms in which music can be embodied. The instances just quoted are minor ones of general application. Of the conceptions in which he is specially indebted to Beethoven, the most important come from the Mass in D. Here the older master, by the very form in which the ideas are cast, had to hold himself in. He was not able to give them the significance in the Mass, which is perfectly proper in great music dramas; and this enlarging and widening of the poetic conception,—this splendor in which it is portrayed,—not only justifies the course of his follower in adopting it, but also calls attention anew to the commanding genius to whom such things are possible.

Some of Wagner's most entrancing effects have their origin in Beethoven. His method of using the violins and flutes in the highest register in prolonged notes, as in the Lohengrin Prelude, and in general when portraying celestial music, are obtained from this source. The Mass in D gives several instances where this idea is presented, not by harp (the customary way), but as Wagner has done in Lohengrin, by the violins and wood-winds in the highest register, beginning pianissimo, gradually descending and augmenting in volume and sonority as the picturing merges from spiritual to worldly concerns. Beethoven's work abounds in intellectual subtleties of this kind. Wagner is sometimes credited with having originated this method for the portrayal of celestial music. Mr. Louis C. Elson says: "Wagner, alone, of all the great masters, does not use the harp for celestial tone coloring, but violins and wood-winds, in prolonged notes in the highest positions. Schumann, Berlioz, Saint-Saens, in fact all the modern tone colorists who have given celestial pictures, use the harp in them, purely because of the association of ideas which come to us from the Scriptures, and this association of the harp with heaven and the angels, only came about because the instrument was the most developed possessed by man at the time the sacred book was written. Wagner's tone coloring is intrinsically the more ecstatic.... Wagner is the first who has broken through this harp conventionality."

In the Wagner-Liszt correspondence, Wagner states that the Lohengrin Prelude typifies choirs of angels bearing the Holy Grail to earth. This idea and the method of its development can be found in the symphonic thought which follows the Preludium to the Benedictus of the Beethoven Mass.

It will be necessary to make a short digression and explain a portion of the canon of the Mass to enable the reader to understand what follows. During the office of the Eucharist the celebrant repeats certain prayers inaudible to the congregation. These begin during the latter part of the Sanctus, which immediately precedes the Benedictus, and are connected with the ceremony of the consecration of the Host. A part of them are conducted in absolute silence. The choir is not required to be silent during all the prayers said by the celebrant, and the occasion is frequently utilized, particularly at high festivals, by the introduction of orchestral music or a brilliant chorus. The choir is silent during the elevation of the Host and chalice, which takes place immediately after the consecration. It is a period of peculiar solemnity, the congregation kneeling in silent prayer at the signal of a gong. After the consecration the priest elevates the Host and chalice, and with the people still kneeling, offers up a prayer silently, the conclusion of which is as follows: "We most humbly beseech Thee, Almighty God, command these things to be carried by the hands of Thy holy angels to Thy altar on high, in the sight of Thy Divine Majesty, that as many as shall partake of the most sacred body and blood of Thy Son at this altar may be filled with every heavenly grace and blessing." The central thought of this prayer is that the sacred elements are borne to heaven by invisible hands.

In the Beethoven Mass a Preludium for orchestra is introduced, to fill in the interval while the celebrant is occupied with these silent prayers. It is an innovation, showing how thoroughly alive Beethoven was to the development of every phase of his subject. Ordinarily, no provision is made for this by the composer, the organist being permitted the privilege of interpolating hymns like the O Salutaris or the Tantum ergo. The Preludium is so timed that it ends at the conclusion of the prayer we have quoted, when the sacred elements are in heaven and are about being returned to earth. It is at this point that the symphonic thought begins, which at the first bar calls to mind celestial harmonies. Here we have the tone-figure, as in the Lohengrin Prelude, given by the violins and flutes in the highest register, beginning in faintest pianissimo. At the second bar the melody begins to descend, being augmented in force by the gradual addition of the more powerful instruments as well as voices when the elements are again on earth. The Lohengrin Prelude has the same idea, but it is developed to a greater extent, with a richer orchestration, the idea being carried to greater length, and rendered more significant in every way, as befits its dramatic character. In both cases, however, the orchestral figure is introduced by the same instruments, and in much the same manner.

The Mass in D furnishes another instance where the celestial harmonies are introduced to still better purpose than in the Benedictus. It is in that portion of the Credo, beginning with the Et incarnatus. The delicate ethereal nature of this music, as indicated by the violins and flutes in the highest positions, is so transcendental, so imbued with spirituality, as almost to evade analysis. By the magic of Beethoven's art the impression is conveyed that the listener overhears far-off angel voices from other spheres, when the heavens were opened for the descent of the Son of God to earth. The instruments give out the merest intimations of sound, scintillations that suggest it rather. In the opening bars of the movement, just before the introduction of this tone-figure, he uses an ancient ecclesiastical style, the Plagal, a mode that obtained centuries before Palestrina. Harsh and strident, inharmonious, are the tones, which in the opening Adagio typify the dread, the foreboding and dismay, that can be supposed to have been felt by the Son of God when the time came to give up a beatific state and enter on the actualities of earthly existence. The sin of the world is already being borne in anticipation. Suddenly we are in the midst of celestial harmonies, delicate gradations and mergings of tones, subtleties of expression, ethereal, evanescent, that come faintly at first on the senses, giving us revelations of spiritual heights, of transcendent states and conditions of the soul. Mankind is here afforded a glimpse beyond the veil. These strains continue until the words *et homo factus est* (and was made man) are reached. At this point the melodies are suddenly cut off, the doors are closed, and we are excluded from further participation in things not meant for mortal ears. A change of tonality and time further accentuates the changed conditions that prevail as the story goes through the

George Alexander Fischer

events of the crucifixion, death and burial of Christ.[I]

[I] Beethoven's love of strongly defined contrasts is nowhere better illustrated than here. The sharp discordant tones, which characterize the opening bars of the movement, are simply pushed aside by the new. It is the subjugation of the worldly by the spiritual, of suffering by happiness.

The Mass in D can be said to be the parent of some of the Parsifal music. Wagner had the discernment to seize on the intellectual subtleties he found there, and to put them to happiest uses. If we compare the instrumental effects just noted with the exquisitely delicate music that opens the Parsifal Prelude after the introductory *leit motif*, we find a solution to each, as well as an affinity, in the religious mysticism in which each is enveloped. There is a central theme, but so shadowy and unreal as to be hardly apparent. Like a nimbus these shimmerings of sound from the violins surround and permeate it, so that one is not aware of any particular melody, but rather it is perceived that the atmosphere is full of a divine melody, as if by spiritual insight the listener had attained to a state of mind akin to that of the seer, and had, for the time being, become one with the composer. The effect is produced of being in the presence of something holy.

The *Naturlangsamkeit* necessary to the birth of any great art-work sometimes extends to its recognition and appreciation by the public. Beethoven considered the Mass in D his greatest achievement, but it gains ground very slowly. It is rarely mentioned, and seldom performed. Similarly Bach's greatest works slumbered nearly a century until brought to light by Mendelssohn.

It is significant that Wagner was as world-weary from middle-age on as was Beethoven. Like him he took refuge in creative work. Both were pioneers, always in advance of their time, cheerfully making the sacrifices which this position entails, diverging ever more and more with advancing years from beaten paths and the ideas of others on the subject of their art. Resignation and asceticism, the goal of mankind, was Wagner's solution of the problem of existence, a conclusion arrived at after reading Schopenhauer. Beethoven had also come to it long before reaching middle-age. Wagner was, in his later years, a mystic, as was Beethoven; and like Beethoven his most congenial work in those years was of a religious character.

George Alexander Fischer

Choose from Thousands of 1stWorldLibrary Classics By

A. M. Barnard
Ada Leverson
Adolphus William Ward
Aesop
Agatha Christie
Alexander Aaronsohn
Alexander Kielland
Alexandre Dumas
Alfred Gatty
Alfred Ollivant
Alice Duer Miller
Alice Turner Curtis
Alice Dunbar
Allen Chapman
Alleyne Ireland
Ambrose Bierce
Amelia E. Barr
Amory H. Bradford
Andrew Lang
Andrew McFarland Davis
Andy Adams
Angela Brazil
Anna Alice Chapin
Anna Sewell
Annie Besant
Annie Hamilton Donnell
Annie Payson Call
Annie Roe Carr
Annonaymous
Anton Chekhov
Archibald Lee Fletcher
Arnold Bennett
Arthur C. Benson
Arthur Conan Doyle
Arthur M. Winfield
Arthur Ransome
Arthur Schnitzler
Arthur Train
Atticus
B.H. Baden-Powell
B. M. Bower
B. C. Chatterjee
Baroness Emmuska Orczy
Baroness Orczy
Basil King
Bayard Taylor
Ben Macomber
Bertha Muzzy Bower
Bjornstjerne Bjornson

Booth Tarkington
Boyd Cable
Bram Stoker
C. Collodi
C. E. Orr
C. M. Ingleby
Carolyn Wells
Catherine Parr Traill
Charles A. Eastman
Charles Amory Beach
Charles Dickens
Charles Dudley Warner
Charles Farrar Browne
Charles Ives
Charles Kingsley
Charles Klein
Charles Hanson Towne
Charles Lathrop Pack
Charles Romyn Dake
Charles Whibley
Charles Willing Beale
Charlotte M. Braeme
Charlotte M. Yonge
Charlotte Perkins Stetson
Clair W. Hayes
Clarence Day Jr.
Clarence E. Mulford
Clemence Housman
Confucius
Coningsby Dawson
Cornelis DeWitt Wilcox
Cyril Burleigh
D. H. Lawrence
Daniel Defoe
David Garnett
Dinah Craik
Don Carlos Janes
Donald Keyhoe
Dorothy Kilner
Dougan Clark
Douglas Fairbanks
E. Nesbit
E. P. Roe
E. Phillips Oppenheim
E. S. Brooks
Earl Barnes
Edgar Rice Burroughs
Edith Van Dyne
Edith Wharton

Edward Everett Hale
Edward J. O'Biren
Edward S. Ellis
Edwin L. Arnold
Eleanor Atkins
Eleanor Hallowell Abbott
Eliot Gregory
Elizabeth Gaskell
Elizabeth McCracken
Elizabeth Von Arnim
Ellem Key
Emerson Hough
Emilie F. Carlen
Emily Bronte
Emily Dickinson
Enid Bagnold
Enilor Macartney Lane
Erasmus W. Jones
Ernie Howard Pie
Ethel May Dell
Ethel Turner
Ethel Watts Mumford
Eugene Sue
Eugenie Foa
Eugene Wood
Eustace Hale Ball
Evelyn Everett-green
Everard Cotes
F. H. Cheley
F. J. Cross
F. Marion Crawford
Fannie E. Newberry
Federick Austin Ogg
Ferdinand Ossendowski
Fergus Hume
Florence A. Kilpatrick
Fremont B. Deering
Francis Bacon
Francis Darwin
Frances Hodgson Burnett
Frances Parkinson Keyes
Frank Gee Patchin
Frank Harris
Frank Jewett Mather
Frank L. Packard
Frank V. Webster
Frederic Stewart Isham
Frederick Trevor Hill
Frederick Winslow Taylor

Friedrich Kerst
Friedrich Nietzsche
Fyodor Dostoyevsky
G.A. Henty
G.K. Chesterton
Gabrielle E. Jackson
Garrett P. Serviss
Gaston Leroux
George A. Warren
George Ade
Geroge Bernard Shaw
George Cary Eggleston
George Durston
George Ebers
George Eliot
George Gissing
George MacDonald
George Meredith
George Orwell
George Sylvester Viereck
George Tucker
George W. Cable
George Wharton James
Gertrude Atherton
Gordon Casserly
Grace E. King
Grace Gallatin
Grace Greenwood
Grant Allen
Guillermo A. Sherwell
Gulielma Zollinger
Gustav Flaubert
H. A. Cody
H. B. Irving
H. C. Bailey
H. G. Wells
H. H. Munro
H. Irving Hancock
H. R. Naylor
H. Rider Haggard
H. W. C. Davis
Haldeman Julius
Hall Caine
Hamilton Wright Mabie
Hans Christian Andersen
Harold Avery
Harold McGrath
Harriet Beecher Stowe
Harry Castlemon
Harry Coghill
Harry Houidini

Hayden Carruth
Helent Hunt Jackson
Helen Nicolay
Hendrik Conscience
Hendy David Thoreau
Henri Barbusse
Henrik Ibsen
Henry Adams
Henry Ford
Henry Frost
Henry James
Henry Jones Ford
Henry Seton Merriman
Henry W Longfellow
Herbert A. Giles
Herbert Carter
Herbert N. Casson
Herman Hesse
Hildegard G. Frey
Homer
Honore De Balzac
Horace B. Day
Horace Walpole
Horatio Alger Jr.
Howard Pyle
Howard R. Garis
Hugh Lofting
Hugh Walpole
Humphry Ward
Ian Maclaren
Inez Haynes Gillmore
Irving Bacheller
Isabel Cecilia Williams
Isabel Hornibrook
Israel Abrahams
Ivan Turgenev
J. G.Austin
J. Henri Fabre
J. M. Barrie
J. M. Walsh
J. Macdonald Oxley
J. R. Miller
J. S. Fletcher
J. S. Knowles
J. Storer Clouston
J. W. Duffield
Jack London
Jacob Abbott
James Allen
James Andrews
James Baldwin

James Branch Cabell
James DeMille
James Joyce
James Lane Allen
James Lane Allen
James Oliver Curwood
James Oppenheim
James Otis
James R. Driscoll
Jane Abbott
Jane Austen
Jane L. Stewart
Janet Aldridge
Jens Peter Jacobsen
Jerome K. Jerome
Jessie Graham Flower
John Buchan
John Burroughs
John Cournos
John F. Kennedy
John Gay
John Glasworthy
John Habberton
John Joy Bell
John Kendrick Bangs
John Milton
John Philip Sousa
John Taintor Foote
Jonas Lauritz Idemil Lie
Jonathan Swift
Joseph A. Altsheler
Joseph Carey
Joseph Conrad
Joseph E. Badger Jr
Joseph Hergesheimer
Joseph Jacobs
Jules Vernes
Julian Hawthrone
Julie A Lippmann
Justin Huntly McCarthy
Kakuzo Okakura
Karle Wilson Baker
Kate Chopin
Kenneth Grahame
Kenneth McGaffey
Kate Langley Bosher
Kate Langley Bosher
Katherine Cecil Thurston
Katherine Stokes
L. A. Abbot
L. T. Meade

L. Frank Baum
Latta Griswold
Laura Dent Crane
Laura Lee Hope
Laurence Housman
Lawrence Beasley
Leo Tolstoy
Leonid Andreyev
Lewis Carroll
Lewis Sperry Chafer
Lilian Bell
Lloyd Osbourne
Louis Hughes
Louis Joseph Vance
Louis Tracy
Louisa May Alcott
Lucy Fitch Perkins
Lucy Maud Montgomery
Luther Benson
Lydia Miller Middleton
Lyndon Orr
M. Corvus
M. H. Adams
Margaret E. Sangster
Margret Howth
Margaret Vandercook
Margaret W. Hungerford
Margret Penrose
Maria Edgeworth
Maria Thompson Daviess
Mariano Azuela
Marion Polk Angellotti
Mark Overton
Mark Twain
Mary Austin
Mary Catherine Crowley
Mary Cole
Mary Hastings Bradley
Mary Roberts Rinehart
Mary Rowlandson
M. Wollstonecraft Shelley
Maud Lindsay
Max Beerbohm
Myra Kelly
Nathaniel Hawthrone
Nicolo Machiavelli
O. F. Walton
Oscar Wilde
Owen Johnson
P.G. Wodehouse
Paul and Mabel Thorne

Paul G. Tomlinson
Paul Severing
Percy Brebner
Percy Keese Fitzhugh
Peter B. Kyne
Plato
Quincy Allen
R. Derby Holmes
R. L. Stevenson
R. S. Ball
Rabindranath Tagore
Rahul Alvares
Ralph Bonehill
Ralph Henry Barbour
Ralph Victor
Ralph Waldo Emmerson
Rene Descartes
Ray Cummings
Rex Beach
Rex E. Beach
Richard Harding Davis
Richard Jefferies
Richard Le Gallienne
Robert Barr
Robert Frost
Robert Gordon Anderson
Robert L. Drake
Robert Lansing
Robert Lynd
Robert Michael Ballantyne
Robert W. Chambers
Rosa Nouchette Carey
Rudyard Kipling
Saint Augustine
Samuel B. Allison
Samuel Hopkins Adams
Sarah Bernhardt
Sarah C. Hallowell
Selma Lagerlof
Sherwood Anderson
Sigmund Freud
Standish O'Grady
Stanley Weyman
Stella Benson
Stella M. Francis
Stephen Crane
Stewart Edward White
Stijn Streuvels
Swami Abhedananda
Swami Parmananda
T. S. Ackland

T. S. Arthur
The Princess Der Ling
Thomas A. Janvier
Thomas A Kempis
Thomas Anderton
Thomas Bailey Aldrich
Thomas Bulfinch
Thomas De Quincey
Thomas Dixon
Thomas H. Huxley
Thomas Hardy
Thomas More
Thornton W. Burgess
U. S. Grant
Upton Sinclair
Valentine Williams
Various Authors
Vaughan Kester
Victor Appleton
Victor G. Durham
Victoria Cross
Virginia Woolf
Wadsworth Camp
Walter Camp
Walter Scott
Washington Irving
Wilbur Lawton
Wilkie Collins
Willa Cather
Willard F. Baker
William Dean Howells
William le Queux
W. Makepeace Thackeray
William W. Walter
William Shakespeare
Winston Churchill
Yei Theodora Ozaki
Yogi Ramacharaka
Young E. Allison
Zane Grey

www.ingramcontent.com/pod-product-compliance
Lightning Source LLC
Chambersburg PA
CBHW030302180626
46810CB00003B/893